Parenting
Your
Toddler

Parenting Your Toddler

THE EXPERT'S GUIDE TO THE TOUGH AND TENDER YEARS

▼ ▼

Patricia H. Shimm

**Associate Director,
Barnard College Center for
Toddler Development**

and *Kate Ballen*

Illustrations by Amy Shimm

Da Capo
∞
LIFE
LONG

A Member of the Perseus Books Group

The anecdotes in this book come from interviews with parents. The names, however, are fictional to preserve the families' anonymity.

Library of Congress Cataloging-in-Publication Data

Shimm, Patricia H. (Patricia Henderson)
    Parenting your toddler : the expert's guide to the tough and tender years / Patricia H. Shimm and Kate Ballen ; illustrations by Amy Shimm.
        p.   cm.
    Includes index.
    ISBN 0-201-62298-X
    1. Toddlers.   2. Parenting.   3. Child rearing.   I. Ballen, Kate.   II. Title.
HQ774.5.S55   1995
649'.123—dc20   94-23148
                                                                                   CIP

Published by Da Capo Press, A member of the Perseus Books Group

Cover design by Suzanne Heiser
Cover photograph © Telegraph Colour Library/FPG
Text design by Karen Savary
Set in 11-point Adobe Garamond by Pagesetters Inc.

▼ ▼ ▼ ▼ ▼ ▼ ▼ ▼ ▼ ▼ ▼ ▼ ▼ ▼ ▼ ▼ ▼ ▼ ▼

To our families with love:
Bob, Joey, Yoko, Peter, and Amy;
Jimmy, Isobel, and Olivia.

CONTENTS

▼ ▼ ▼ ▼ ▼ ▼ ▼ ▼ ▼ ▼ ▼ ▼ ▼ ▼ ▼ ▼ ▼ ▼ ▼ ▼

ACKNOWLEDGMENTS

▼ ▼ ▼ ▼ ▼ ▼ ▼ ▼ ▼ ▼ ▼ ▼ ▼ ▼ ▼ ▼ ▼ ▼ ▼ ▼

THIS BOOK WOULDN'T HAVE BEEN WRITTEN WITHOUT THE hundreds of toddlers and parents who passed through Barnard's College Center for Toddler Development sharing their feelings, experience, and ideas. We owe them our greatest debt. Among the many parents who have patiently and generously given their time for this book are Ellen Abrams, Eleanor Adam, Elsie Adams, Alison Anthoine, Rajeswari Ayer, Sian Ballen, Carol Berner, Andi Bernstein, Lakshmi Bloom, Dr. Ivan Bresky, Denise Demong, Chris Garrett, Carla Glasser, David Glasser, Dr. Sezelle Haddon, Marta Hallett, Leah Keith, Lynda Koplewicz, Barbara Landau, Ruth Lazarus, Stephanie Mahlman, Judith Melinger, Gay McIntosh, Susan Morgenthau, Chris Pendry, Channing Redford, James Rosenthal, Julie Sakellariadis, Barbara Wallner, Dolly Williams, and Lori Zabar.

We also wish to thank our collegues at Barnard's Toddler Center who have contributed invaluable feedback and encouragement: Dr. J. Lawrence Aber, Dr. Kathleen Deane, Tricia Hanley Ettenger, Emma Forbes-Jones, Stephanie Jones, Pamela Morris, Leslie Ross, and Barbara Salander.

Others who have been generous with their time and expertise: Irving and Natalie Ballen, Sylvia Cohn, Peter Felcher, Ellen Germain, Lucienne Giardino, Ellen Goldsmith, Sue Nager, Jaclyn Paré, Freddie Pomerance, Arthur Rosenthal, Ellen Rosenthal, Judith Willingham Shimm, and Dr. Michael Traister.

Special gratitude to our editor, Nancy Miller, who always endorsed this project with enthusiasm and to our agent, Carla Glasser, who wholeheartedly participated in this book every sentence of the way.

And, finally, thanks to Robert Shimm and Jim Rosenthal, whose love and support inspired us throughout the writing of the book.

▼ ▼ ▼ ▼ ▼ ▼ ▼ ▼ ▼ ▼ ▼ ▼ ▼ ▼ ▼ ▼ ▼ ▼ ▼

TODDLERS HAVE BEEN THE MAIN FOCUS OF MY WORLD for over twenty years. I know them, I feel I understand them, I love them. As associate director of the Barnard College Center for Toddler Development, I've been surrounded by toddlers, their parents, their teachers, their caregivers, and psychologists who study them. This book is the result of two decades of collective wisdom.

In 1973, I helped the late Dr. Frances Fuchs Schacter start Barnard's Center for Toddler Development. The Center was one of the first programs to focus totally on the toddler years, from around one and a half to three years of age. Our school has since become the prototype for toddler programs across the United States. The purpose of the Toddler Center, which is based in Barnard's psychology department, is to be a unique first school experience for toddlers and families, to give undergraduate students an opportunity to work with this age group, and to contribute to early childhood research. When Dr. J. Lawrence Aber became the director in 1980, the Center also became nationally known for its research. An offshoot of the program has been that the Center's strategies and approaches can be used by parents and caregivers at home.

In *Parenting Your Toddler* we've gathered together the voices of toddlers to recreate a real picture of what a toddler feels and acts like. We've also tried to respond to parents' concerns and enable them not only to be sensitive but also to rejoice in these significant years when, for the first time, a child sees herself as an independent person, separate from her mother and father.

Many parents perceive toddlerhood as the terrible twos, but there is another side to this complex period. A toddler is also feisty, curious, enthusiastic, opinionated, interested, persistent, and yes, even reasonable, and a totally affectionate and sociable human being. I've tried to provide practical advice on what to say and do in the widest possible variety of situations in a toddler's life.

Right from the start, parents and caregivers have been an essential part of the Center's program. (My coauthor, Kate Ballen, is a two-time Toddler Center parent.) The grown-ups stay at the Center during the opening month and participate in the slow separation process. Throughout the year, parents continue to share their views and concerns in weekly parent groups. They are also active participants in the Center's research and are interviewed about their memories of childhood and views on parenting a toddler-aged child. A unique feature of the Center is a one-way vision room, where the grown-ups have the opportunity to observe their toddlers in the playgroup.

Parents learn firsthand from watching their toddler play. They gain a new understanding of what it is like to be in a toddler world. He's angry, he hits. She wants a toy, she takes. She sits down for a snack of rice cakes, she grabs the whole tray. He gets his shirt wet, he refuses even to consider a dry one. She sees a chair she wants, she pushes the occupant off her throne. On the other hand, if he sees one of his buddies crying, he can become the picture of empathy and sensitivity. Either he'll join in crying or he will stay near the crier just to watch and give her the support she doesn't want. It's always a great relief for parents to see that even when their toddler flings herself at their feet begging them not to leave, within ten minutes she is usually involved in the activities of the room.

Most importantly, parents at last can see by looking through this one-way mirror that there is a wide range of behavior in normal toddler development—from shy and retiring to the aggressive baby, sumo wrestler style.

Our program's philosophy is based on the work of the Swiss psychologist Jean Piaget. He believed that children learn through their own active exploration, with little interference from grown-ups. Twice a week, two groups of twelve children ranging from eighteen to thirty-six months come to the Center for a two-and-a-half-hour playgroup. The group is run by me, professional teacher Leslie Ross, and undergraduate student teachers. While our teachers select what toys are on the shelves—puzzles, play dough, blocks—the key is that each toddler has the freedom to select what he wants to play with. There are very few group activities because we want every child to play at his own pace and ability. The next time you take your toddler to a birthday party and want her to sit in a circle like everyone else, remember that it is totally age appropriate for her to be running around finding her own entertainment.

Over the years, grabbing, hitting, pushing, fighting have become part of the definition of the word *socialization* here at the Toddler Center. We have found that this assertive behavior is normal.

When my three children were growing up, we believed we had to raise well-mannered, obedient citizens. We expected our toddlers always to share, never to hit, and to say "thank you" for everything. We at the Center realize that this is the time for a two-year-old to assert and test his parents so that he can become a separate person. He'll adopt the positive social graces of his culture at a later time in his development.

We've learned never to use the word *share* at the Center—it is useless. You just can't expect toddlers to be magnanimous, because very few understand that all possessions do not belong to them. Instead, we concentrate on how warring toddlers can communicate their feelings and negotiate a peaceful settlement. For instance, when Molly refuses to share her train with Alex, we explain what she's feeling and then suggest that Molly may finish playing soon. Meanwhile, we give Alex a substitute toy while he's waiting his turn. "I see you like playing with that train by yourself. When you are finished, give it to Alex. Alex, here's a ball to play with."

On playdates it can be a great help for parents to have doubles of popular toys. It also can be helpful if the other child brings over some of his favorite toys. But please don't feel you are raising a selfish scrooge if your toddler refuses to hand over his toys with a smile. By the golden age of three, most children become more sharing.

We have discovered that potty parties are the in thing for the two-year-old crowd. Potties are lined up in a circle, and anyone who wants to use them can join in the fun. Toddlers sit, grunt, and turn red-faced as they go about their business. Since children really enjoy copying each other, we have found this a painless way to toilet train them. We have also discovered that toddlers will eat almost anything, even a nonglamorous snack of rice cakes and watered-down apple juice, if the adults don't get involved in a power struggle with them.

But above all, we have learned how parents and caregivers can help a toddler express her feelings not only through dramatic play but through language. Once a toddler can recognize her feelings, putting words to them not only helps her master developmental tasks, such as toilet training, sleeping alone, and playing alone, but it gives her an extra dose of self-esteem. "I see you're angry because Sara is going ahead of you on the slide and you wanted to be first," or "Boy, I see you want all the toys in the store. I wish you could have them all."

Throughout our day we acknowledge disgruntled feelings, for example, "I know you really want to be alone in the rocking boat," answer questions immediately, and make educated guesses and interpretations of a toddler's grunts, screams, and whines. For instance, when a toddler points to the art shelf, we might say, "Oh, I see you'd like some crayons to draw with." Acknowledging and interpreting a toddler's feelings really makes him feel that he counts.

What will you find in this book? You will find both our philosophy and practical, hands-on recommendations about toddler issues such as toilet training, eating, sleeping, setting limits, playdates, preparing your child for a new baby, separating, and becoming an individual. We have also included information on such topics as caregivers, working mothers, and not pushing your toddler too hard that can help make life better for both child and parents. This book even has chapters on how to take a guilt-free vacation without your children and on vacationing with the entire family.

We look at these issues from many angles—offering not only step-by-step guidelines but also helpful ways of talking to your toddler and understanding how to promote her independence and confidence. So many toddler accomplishments are extensions of their ability to deal with separation. Over and over again in this book we talk about separation, and by separation we don't mean simply what to say and do when you leave your child with a babysitter. A toddler's ability to play alone and with peers, to use the toilet, and to fall asleep alone, and even his loud, insistent "No!" are signs that your toddler is learning how to stand on his own two feet.

In each chapter we're not shy about discussing our basic themes: following your toddler's lead by not giving him suggestions or changing what he's interested in, setting limits to make her feel safe, and understanding and articulating what he feels.

A very important part of many chapters helps parents review how their own childhoods can influence their current parenting style. For instance, if your parents labeled you the generous, sensitive, considerate firstborn, you might find it hard to deal with a selfish, headstrong toddler. Or if your parents wouldn't tolerate any display of anger, it might be hard to watch your toddler have a tantrum in public over some minor infraction.

All of our advice comes from the experience of dealing with hundreds of toddlers and families over the course of two decades. We have so often heard mothers and fathers say, "I feel so confident at work, but I can't deal with getting my child to sleep at night or to eat the right food." There is nothing more humbling than being a parent. I hope this book helps parents gain the expertise that will enable them to trust and enjoy themselves as competent mothers and fathers.

In the process of trusting ourselves as parents, it's so important to accept and respect your children. When you know your child is scared of clowns, why take her to the circus? When you know he's uncomfortable with large groups of children, why have a big birthday party for him? Remember, your child has years ahead to experiment and enjoy the good things in life. On the other hand, when a toddler wants to run across the street or refuses to sit in a car seat, a parent, of course, must be able to set limits. Following your toddler's cues and being her advocate are essential to helping her flourish.

The most confident children seem to have parents who are able to support their autonomy. What exactly does that mean? It means that when Stephanie wants you to read *Good Night, Moon* for what seems the tenth time in two days, you don't totally take over and say: "Ugh, not again! Can't we read another book? I'm sure you would like this story better." Instead, you follow Stephanie's lead, read the book, and make her think, "Wow, my dad really wants me to enjoy what I like."

Once again, the depth and breadth of this book is the result of two decades of responding to and learning from parents and care-givers, clinical research, and, of course, befriending and listening to the hundreds of toddlers who have attended the Toddler Center. All the anecdotes in the book come from the Toddler Center's population, which includes a mixed group of working and nonworking parents.

*Parenting
Your
Toddler*

▼ ▼ ▼ ▼ ▼ ▼ ▼ ▼ ▼ ▼ ▼ ▼ ▼ ▼ ▼ ▼ ▼ ▼

CHAPTER 1

Socialization

WHEN I THINK OF WHAT SOCIALIZATION MEANS FOR a toddler I always remember the story of a close friend. She brought her two-and-a-half-year-old to work. The toddler took one look at his mother's boss and said: "Hi, doodyhead. How are you, doodyhead?" Fortunately, the boss took the remark for what it was—an inspired comment from a two-and-a-half-year-old and immediately said, "What a creative child you are."

If you expect social graces, charm, and reasonableness from a toddler you are going to be disappointed. Just because a two-and-a-half-year-old walks and talks doesn't mean she is capable of living up to the social standards of the adult world. A toddler truly doesn't understand that other people have rights and that every toy in the world doesn't belong to her. The beginnings of socialization for a two-year-old can be very assertive behavior when her "mine" clashes with the "mine" of every other human being in the world.

But incredible as it can seem, eventually your toddler will become civilized. Through experiences with peers and everyday life encounters with the grocer, the pediatrician, grandparents, and others, a toddler gradually and almost without any help from her parents adopts the social mores of the human race. By around the golden age of three, most children are able to feel for others (some old-fashioned empathy) and at the same time stand up for themselves. In other words, your child becomes socialized.

In the meantime, every family seems to have at least a few stories of being totally embarrassed by a toddler. For example, one mother was taking her almost-three-year-old son on what seemed an uneventful car ride with a neighbor. The rather large woman was full of compliments for the toddler. "You are so adorable. Who'd you get those long eyelashes from? If you come over tomorrow I am going to have a big surprise for you." Finally, after ten minutes of not uttering a sound, sweet, taciturn Peter said slowly and emphatically: "My daddy says you are an elephant." As shocked silence spread through the car, Peter suddenly had a brilliant afterthought and quickly added, "My daddy likes elephants."

It can be hard to accept that acting your age as a toddler means being tyrannical, silly, nonsharing, and aggressive and having emotional swings that could make anyone dizzy. So many parents describe their toddlers along the following lines: "He's rarely polite. Sometimes he'll say hello, sometimes he won't. He screams, laughs, sings at the top of his voice. He wants everything for himself, including the shirt off my back."

If ever there was a time to try to forget about "appropriate" behavior, this is it. Next time your toddler performs what seems the ultimate embarrassment, try saying to yourself: "Wait a minute, where is my sense of humor? Wait a minute, didn't she embarrass me worse yesterday? Wait a minute, this child may be mine but she isn't me!" Even at this early age, try to separate from your toddler (after all, independence is what toddlerhood is about). It is so important for parents not to perceive their toddler through everyone else's eyes. Just as you want your toddler to enjoy and feel for other people, so you want her to feel you enjoy her fully.

▼ ▼ ▼ ▼ ▼ ▼ ▼ ▼ ▼ ▼ ▼ ▼ ▼ ▼ ▼ ▼ ▼ ▼ ▼

This Is How a Toddler Looks and Should Look

1. She isn't going to share, but watch how enraged she gets when her playmates won't share with her.

2. He isn't a reliable greeter. When entering a room, he very well might not say hello. He also hates to leave and will often demonstrate his feelings by having a tantrum.

3. She wants to do absolutely everything herself until one second later she screams, "I need you!"

4. He is very greedy; he wants it all.

5. She isn't going to say no or yes gracefully.

6. He will never think of thanking you or saying "please" unless heavily prompted. (And the truth is, you don't want your toddler to be Mr. or Ms. Manners. At this age he needs to test limits to find himself.)

7. Just when you expect her to kiss, she bites or hits.

8. Just when you expect him to clean up, he pulls everything off the shelves.

9. Just when you think she is becoming reasonable, she throws herself screaming onto the floor.

▲ ▲ ▲ ▲ ▲ ▲ ▲ ▲ ▲ ▲ ▲ ▲ ▲ ▲ ▲ ▲ ▲ ▲ ▲

Share, Share, Share

Is my child selfish, spoiled, and mean spirited because he won't share? Absolutely not. You can't expect toddlers to be generous and altruistic. In fact, I'd be suspicious of a toddler's generosity if he gives everything to friends all the time (it may be his way of controlling a situation). A toddler is exercising his due rights when he holds on with all his might to possessions. Two-year-olds really believe that all property is an extension of themselves. You might even know some adults like that!

At the Toddler Center we try not to use the word *share*. The concept is too advanced for most toddlers because they truly don't understand that all possessions shouldn't belong to them. Very few toddlers are going to freely share without an adult directing the show. Here's an example of how some toddlers interpreted the word *sharing*:

Lily walked into her friend's house and her eyes immediately lit upon a beautiful new doll. Lily quickly said, "Joan, I'll share your doll." Joan, who obviously had heard that sharing was a good thing, replied, "Oh yes, we'll share the doll." Lily then grabbed the doll and ran into a corner with it, saying, "Now, we are sharing." Sharing understood this way means, it's mine, especially since I used the word to get it. Naturally, all the adults were upset with Lily. After all, she had promised to share.

Of course, most parents do use the word *share* with their toddler. But don't expect your child to hand her toys over with a big smile just because you tell her to share. Sometimes she might be willing to be the benevolent bestower of gifts, but very often she won't even consider the idea. During the toddler years, rather than chant "share, share, share," it is more effective to report on your child's feelings while lightly encouraging a little generosity. For example, when Annie won't share her ball with Sam, try saying: "I see you like playing with that ball by yourself. When you are finished, how about giving it to Sam. Meanwhile, Sam, here's some chalk to draw with." These words should be modified to your own style, but the idea is to translate your toddler's actions into feelings.

Sharing really becomes the issue of the hour during playdates when your toddler has a competitor. It can be a great idea to have doubles of some hot toys, such as cash registers or dolls. It can also be helpful for the other child to bring over some of his favorite toys. You just can't expect toddlers to wait their turn. Favorite and new toys might be put away before the playmate arrives. While stashing away the favorite teddy bear, it's important to let your child know that she does not have to share everything. "If you don't want Alex to play with your bear, let's put it away so you don't have to think about it."

Sometimes, much to many parents' mortification, it's not only new and favorite toys that your toddler won't share. He very well might not want to share any toy. (By the way, if your toddler has just become the recipient of a new sibling, he will share colds and chicken pox—but that's about all—with the new baby and other children.) One father remarks: "When my son has a playdate, the other child literally only has to glance at a toy for my son to say, 'That's mine.' Heaven forbid if the other child dares to touch a toy." When it looks as though the playdate has reached this type of standstill it's helpful for parents to have creative solutions on hand, such as finger paints or stickers, to distract the two toddlers and maybe even get them to play together.

It can be hard to accept a toddler's unyielding personality. But this, too, will change. By the time most children are about three years old, they become bona fide sharers because they start to care about winning friends and influencing people. In the meantime, remember that no matter how many times a parent lectures on the virtues of sharing, a toddler will notice if his parent counts every toy brought to the playground ten times and gets upset when another child puts fingerprints on his or her child's shovel. On the other hand, a toddler will also take note if a parent is generous, shares freely, and helps others.

▼ ▼ ▼ ▼ ▼ ▼ ▼ ▼ ▼ ▼ ▼ ▼ ▼ ▼ ▼ ▼ ▼ ▼

How to Get Through the Nonsharing Years

1. Don't expect your toddler to share.

2. Don't overuse the word *share*.

3. Buy doubles of a few popular toys for playdates.

4. Put away special toys before playdates.

5. Be generous yourself.

▲ ▲ ▲ ▲ ▲ ▲ ▲ ▲ ▲ ▲ ▲ ▲ ▲ ▲ ▲ ▲ ▲ ▲ ▲

Playdates

Playdate, a term that didn't even exist when I was a young mother, has become the buzzword for a bit of old-fashioned socializing between children. The purpose of playdates is to give your toddler exposure to other children her own age in a secure environment. I can't think of a better way to move along the process of growing up than for a toddler to spend time with other toddlers.

That said, I wouldn't make the day into one long playdate. Most toddlers can only keep their cool for so long. For this very reason, some parents I know limit their toddler's playdates to one hour or so. When your child first starts having playdates indoors I'd also recommend restricting the date to one other child. Outdoors, where there is a lot more space and diversion, your toddler will be able to handle more than one child.

It would be very nice if your toddler could regularly play and become comfortable with the same circle of children. Once in a while an older or younger child is a welcome change in a toddler's social calendar, but on a regular basis I'd generally stick to his peers. An older child would probably end up giving your toddler too fast an education in socialization—a little too much bossing and bullying. Your toddler might then feel obligated to try out his new street smarts on a younger child who is as defenseless as he feels.

Playdates are also an education for parents. By sitting back you can quickly see how your toddler reacts to other children—pleased, wary, curious, eager, frightened. Of course, your toddler might very well show all these emotions at one time or another. You can also observe different styles of playing.

Many toddlers learn to interact with each other when it seems as though they are not interacting at all. Even if your toddler is generally very outgoing, he may barely acknowledge another child's presence on a playdate. You may see two strangers across a room crowded with toys never once speaking or even glancing at each other. Or they may be in parallel play—standing next to each other but playing as though they are in their own separate bubbles.

Once your toddler steps out of her bubble you may see some follow-the-leader play. One child may totally boss another (and the boss very well may be three months younger). Or you may even see what actually looks like give-and-take play, two toddlers exploring their toys together.

It isn't unusual for a toddler to spend an entire playdate in his parent's lap. While a clingy toddler can make a parent embarrassed and even angry, particularly when the other child seems independent, it is important to show a little empathy. A toddler is just starting to find his own way of interacting. Instead of pushing your toddler out of the nest by saying, "Go play with Suzy," or, "You aren't suppose to sit in my lap when your friends are here," you will help him feel more comfortable by getting him involved with an adult (you). Pick out a toy or book he can't refuse. He might enjoy himself so much that he will forget about you in a few minutes and venture forth. Or he may stay glued in your lap for the entire playdate. But next time at Billy's house you may be surprised to see him run off with Billy or forsake your lap for that of another adult.

All these ways of playing are what adults can expect in the process of a toddler becoming socialized. No one style of play is more normal or better. In fact, you will probably see your toddler try them all out on his playdate rounds. Different toddlers will bring out different aspects of your child's personality.

"Why should you have to kick the ball if I can do it for you?"

How Adults Can Enhance a Playdate

A little bit of benign neglect during a playdate goes a long way toward making a toddler more confident. A grown-up should not initiate all the activities but should be a willing participant if things get out of hand. For example, if your toddler seems to have trouble settling down with her friend on a playdate, why not bring out the play dough and put it on a table with the children facing each other? Just because you bring out the play dough, though, doesn't mean that you should start rolling out stars and cutting clown faces. A parent's job is to set up the environment. Your child's job is to play in it. Every time adults take over a toddler's play, the freedom of a two- or three-year-old is diminished.

Some parents let their toddler almost totally fend for herself on playdates because they believe it will make her more independent. But when a parent barely interacts with his or her child, even though the parent is well intentioned, the toddler can easily feel that her actions don't count and shut down. For example, if your child doesn't talk very much, why not venture a guess as to the meaning of his grunts and gestures? When he points to a block set on a shelf you can say: "Oh, I see you want to play with those blocks. Let me help you get them down." You want your toddler to feel that someone is responding to him. By taking an educated guess at what your child wants and articulating his thoughts out loud, you help him feel understood.

At this age the key to seeing what your toddler is feeling is through her dramatic play. This is an ideal time to be her spokesperson and interpreter. For example, Eliza, who just had a new sister, was very intently feeding a doll with a bottle when she suddenly threw the doll on the floor and shouted, "No!" Her mother quickly interpreted: "Boy, babies can take up a lot of Mommy's and Daddy's time when they have to be fed. Sometimes Eliza has to wait around for her story time. I bet that could make her angry."

While playdates give parents the benefit of another adult's company, don't expect your toddlers to go off quietly into a room and play together. Sip your coffee and have an adult conversation, but sit near where the children are playing. A toddler will usually wander back to her parents every so often for reassurance. Says one mother: "My friend and I were so eager to have some time alone together that our hopes were too high. We would walk our two-and-a-half-year-olds into the bedroom and then make a mad dash for the kitchen. Guess what? Every two minutes or so one of them would come out sobbing and screaming for one of us. In retrospect, this explains why the playdates were such disasters."

How messy do you allow a playdate to get? Parents have a variety of tolerance levels for mess. If you know you can't stand having things out of order, have the playdate in your child's room so that there is only one room to clean up. Restrict all the mushy, gushy activities, like playing with play dough and painting, to the kitchen. If it drives you crazy to watch the children dive into new activities without straightening up, incorporate cleanup time at the end of each activity. Don't ask if they want to clean up, but instead start the ball rolling by putting the toys on the shelf while singing "It's time to clean up." I've rarely met a toddler who doesn't like to clean up to a song. But keep in mind, an adult is going to have to be the major supervisor and cleaner at this age.

The best playdates seem to occur when the grown-ups like each other. If the adults aren't enjoying each other, it won't be a relaxed, happy atmosphere for anyone. Toddlers often naturally seem to become best friends with their parents' best friends' children.

But no matter how much you might relish the other adult's company, if his or her child always seems to be fighting it's time to review the match. Just as parents have different tolerances for mess, they also have different reactions to children hitting each other. At the Toddler Center when children are fighting over material goods, if they are basically equals in strength and size, we let it go to the natural end—someone wins the toy. However, if one child seems to be hitting for no reason at all and the victim is always your son or daughter I'd halt the playdates and try again in a few months. When the children turn three and are more willing to share, they might even become best friends.

If you are the parent of a toddler who is aggressive, try staying near her and redirecting her aggression. Even though she may act like the warrior of the toddler world, she very well could be fearful of the other child. Getting to the root of her feelings may help dissolve her fierceness. "I don't think Jimmy likes to be hit. If you are angry, hit this hammer toy. I think maybe you really want to play with Jimmy. It looks like he would like to play with you in the sandbox now." Rushing your toddler from playdate to playdate or class to class, could also be a cause of aggression. She may have a classic case of burnout and may feel overwhelmed by so many new situations. She may need time just to sit quietly and play at her own pace.

▼ ▼ ▼ ▼ ▼ ▼ ▼ ▼ ▼ ▼ ▼ ▼ ▼ ▼ ▼ ▼ ▼ ▼ ▼

Activities for Playdates

Try making the environment on a playdate as simple as possible so that toddlers have room to discover without feeling overwhelmed. Below are some popular activities.

1. **Tent.** Drape a tablecloth over a table. Put blankets, flashlights, and some books inside the tent.

2. **Easel.** Tape a sheet of paper on the refrigerator and place some newspaper on the floor.

3. **Large boxes.** For drawing, playing store, or just crawling through.

4. **Puzzles.**

5. **Housekeeping corner.** Dress-up clothes, dolls, cars, telephones, brooms and dustpans.

6. **Art table.** Table and chairs with crayons, play dough, and stickers to decorate bags or cups.

7. **Tape recorder.** Music for singing and dancing.

▲ ▲ ▲ ▲ ▲ ▲ ▲ ▲ ▲ ▲ ▲ ▲ ▲ ▲ ▲ ▲ ▲ ▲ ▲

The Bully and the Wimp

Some children come out of babyhood with a firm stance and a raucous laugh and grab everything and everyone in sight. You could tell this type of child to stop half a dozen times and she'll keep testing. Another type of child seems very shy, walks with gingerly steps, and, if anyone comes within touching range, gives away his toy and cries at the drop of a hat.

How can parents know if their toddler is going in the right direction in becoming more socialized? Once again, socialization to me means concern for others and being able to take care of your own needs. In truth, it really is hard to see if your toddler is progressing. Both the aggressive and the shy toddler try out different personalities. One moment he can show great empathy for a crying friend and the next minute he can bite her like a tiger and grab her toys like a thief.

All this personality flucuation can sometimes make parents feel as though they are raising Dr. Jekyll and Mr. Hyde. But most toddlers do fluctuate from being aggressive grabbers and hitters to tentative, sensitive children who always seem to have their feelings hurt.

So how do you help a child who is feeling less assertive to be secure and strong when he is playing with other children? And how do you show him the softer side of himself when he is aggressive? To put it bluntly, we are talking about bullies and wimps. A bully at this age, like Oz's tin man, needs a heart, and a wimp, like Oz's lion, needs courage.

With the less assertive toddler, the name of the game is empowerment. Use simple dialogue to help him feel that he can take care of himself. If you see an aggressive toddler pulling his teddy bear away from him, give him words that help him stand up for himself. You can encourage him to hold on by saying: "Hold on tight. Tell Jason, 'It's mine.' "

What about the toddler who will stop at nothing to get everything for herself? Underneath this big-shot attitude is usually a sensitive child who can be in just as much pain as the victim. It can be hard sometimes to refrain from yelling and screaming at her. But instead of embarrassing her by saying, "Give that toy right back. We share here," how about saying, "Gee, Julie, I see you need every toy in this room. When you're finished, give it back"? Then wait a minute before asking, "Are you finished?"

While sometimes all this talking can feel simplistic and overdone, I've repeatedly seen both cautious and aggressive toddlers flourish when given words by understanding parents. Empathy helps build a toddler's self-esteem.

▼ ▼ ▼ ▼ ▼ ▼ ▼ ▼ ▼ ▼ ▼ ▼ ▼ ▼ ▼ ▼ ▼ ▼ ▼

Bully and Wimp

The dialogue below is an example of how a parent can empower both the aggressive and the cautious toddler. The parent shows in a nonjudgmental way that he or she understands how the child is feeling and then gives the child words so that she can express her own feelings.

Bully: Give me that bucket now. I need it now. (Without waiting a second she grabs the bucket from Matthew and runs away.)

Parent: Sara, I see you took that bucket that Matthew was playing with.

Bully: I want it.

Parent: As soon as you are finished, give it back.

Bully: No, I need it.

Parent: I know you need it. But will you be finished soon? (By asking the aggressor if she's finished, the parent is giving her a chance to save face and give back the toy.)

Parent (to victim): Say, "It's mine." You can be angry Sara took your bucket. Next time hold on tight and say, "It's mine." You can tell her.

What usually happens at this point is that the aggressor throws the toy to the victim. She isn't made to feel ashamed, so she can show a little empathy for others. Meanwhile, the satisfied victim gets a glimmer of understanding: "Hey, I can handle this. It does work to hold on."

▲ ▲ ▲ ▲ ▲ ▲ ▲ ▲ ▲ ▲ ▲ ▲ ▲ ▲ ▲ ▲ ▲ ▲ ▲

Biters and Hitters

You have to stop a child from hurting other people. Not only can biting and hitting be painful, but your toddler will also start to feel bad because no one will want to play with him anymore.

Remember, you don't have a monster just because your toddler bites or hits. Neither is a cardinal sin. Biting didn't start out as an antisocial activity. It's a natural progression from sucking, gumming, hugging. Your toddler also really might not know that socking someone on the arm is not an appropriate way to greet people.

If parents don't overreact, a toddler will probably have a short career as a biter and hitter. Try saying calmly and seriously: "I can't let you hurt Caroline. But I will also not let anyone hurt you. You can tell me when you are angry."

If your child can't stop hitting or biting, remove him from the proximity of the other child and possibly the room. If you find that your child is getting a reputation for being a slugger, you'll have to step in even more. For example, before going to a playdate let your child know that if he hits or bites you will take him home. This is an example of setting firm limits for a toddler.

It can be difficult to be the parent of a child who is always being aggressive. Sometimes parents are so embarrassed that their first instinct is to run out of the room as quickly as possible without offering an apology. This action can enrage the other parent, who may think that you don't care. Better to err on the side of giving an apology. More often than not you'll hear: "I understand. Sometimes these things just happen."

It can also be very difficult to refrain from scolding someone else's child if she is aggressive. First-time parents, in particular, can think a child is seriously bad when she hits their toddler. But scolding someone else's child does nothing helpful for your toddler. It's more important for you to pay attention to how your toddler is feeling as the victim. Also, if you want to remain friends with the other child's parents, remember that interfering with their child is a sure way to cause bad feelings.

▼ ▼ ▼ ▼ ▼ ▼ ▼ ▼ ▼ ▼ ▼ ▼ ▼ ▼ ▼ ▼ ▼ ▼ ▼ ▼

Quick Lines to Remember in a Pinch

1. To the hitter: "I can't let you hurt anyone and no one will hurt you."

2. To the bully: "I see you want that ball. When you are finished, give it back. . . . Are you finished yet?"

3. To the wimp: "Hold on tight. Say, 'It's mine.' "

4. To the want-it-all child: "I see you want it all. I wish you could have every toy in this room."

5. To the child who constantly wants to be carried: "Up, up, down." (Grant her half a wish. Make a brief game of picking her up and then putting her down.)

▲ ▲ ▲ ▲ ▲ ▲ ▲ ▲ ▲ ▲ ▲ ▲ ▲ ▲ ▲ ▲ ▲ ▲ ▲ ▲

How Parents' Attitudes Affect Socialization

It's natural for different parents to be biased in different social situations. Imagine how some parents feel when they see another child taking a toy from their beloved son. The mother might quickly jump in to defend her child. As she comes to the rescue, she may become enraged at the two-year-old grabber and see him as a psychopath at the beginning of a homicidal career. Could it be that this parent feels like a victim herself, that she thinks that everyone is out to get her?

Another parent may have quite a different reaction to this scene. He's always been afraid to make waves and take sides. He calmly justifies the situation to his son: "You know, sometimes kids want each other's toys. It happens to everyone." This parent was the negotiator in his family. From an early age he decided that anger was nonproductive.

However, the parent of the grabber may feel that her child's aggression isn't all bad. This mother may be proud of her pint-sized toughie, even though she realizes that her child is a bit too rough. This parent may very well use all the right jargon: "I can't let you hurt anyone and no one will hurt you." She then can't understand that these words aren't working because, in her innermost core, she is proud that her toddler is standing so firmly on his own two feet. Why? Maybe this mother has always had a hard time standing up for herself.

If you find yourself getting very hot under the collar about your toddler's behavior, thinking about your past history can help.

Some parents may actually slow down their toddler's socialization because they find themselves resenting the time their toddler spends on playdates or anywhere away from the comfort of her own home. These mothers or fathers may find themselves making excuses (she seems a little tired, it might rain later) when anyone calls for a playdate. This hesitancy about letting their toddler go could mean they have some difficulty with separations. Separation is the most important accomplishment of toddlerhood, so this issue rates a chapter of its own. See Chapter 2 for details.

Parents' Feeling Embarrassed

How many times have you cringed with embarrassment when you've heard your toddler shriek on the playground, "Give me that bear, it's mine," or watched your toddler plant a bite instead of a kiss on your mother-in-law's cheek?

Parents would find so many situations easier if they could only recognize that all this embarrassing behavior is normal and age appropriate. The next step is to rise above the situation, awful as it may feel. (Your mother-in-law really will forgive your toddler; the other parent really won't think your nonsharing child is a monster.) Don't be intimidated by what other people think. Be your child's advocate and try to understand why she may be acting out. What is important is to become the parent you are. What does your toddler need? Why is she behaving like this? Are you embarrassed because once again you aren't looking good in the reflective glory of your toddler? Or because your child is just showing healthy development that is a tad embarrassing? Feeling angry because you are embarrassed is not going to help your toddler.

When you feel embarrassed, discreet as you may think you are being, a toddler usually picks up on it. At a holiday party at the Toddler Center one three-year-old girl blasted out "Jingle Bells" at the top of her voice. The mother was very uncomfortable with her daughter's exuberance and moved quickly away from her to the snack table, almost as if she were leaving the scene of a crime! The child noticed instantly. A toddler may not understand why her actions are embarrassing, but she is able to feel that she's somehow failed her mother or father.

Of course, when your toddler picks up on your feelings of embarrassment it does help him to become socialized. He realizes that he did not conform to society's rules. According to psychologists, it is appropriate for toddlers to feel the emotion of shame. The point is, you don't want your toddler feeling too ashamed of himself too often.

Here are some common embarrassing toddler incidents in which parents can become their child's advocate.

Screaming in Public   When your child is out of control, screaming in a crowded restaurant at the height of lunch hour, you may get some of the dirtiest looks ever directed your way.

Solution: To the hostile audience around you, give a sincere apology. Then, if you can't calm your toddler in five minutes or so, it's better for one and all to say good-bye and retreat to the comfort of your home.

Not Saying Hello   Your toddler hasn't seen her Aunt Jenny in a month. Aunt Jenny arrives at your doorstep with bags of presents and a big "Hello!" But does your darling two-year-old greet her? No, she looks at her feet and then retreats behind your jacket.

Solution: Instead of embarrassing your toddler by saying, "Now say hello and thank Aunt Jenny for the presents" because *you* are embarrassed, what about looking Aunt Jenny straight in the eye and telling her, "Seems like Margo doesn't want to greet you just now. Thank you so much for all the presents. I'm sure in a little while Margo will be able to thank you herself." To Margo I'd add: "I see you don't want to say anything to Aunt Jenny. What about doing it later?"

Making a Scene Over Food   You are taking Richard to his grandmother's for a special lunch. She has cooked and raved about her wonderful coq au vin (known in less rarified circles as chicken in the pot) for days. Richard takes one look at her gourmet meal and instantly says: "Yuck, no like. I want peanut butter and jelly."

Solution: Turn directly to the grandmother and say wholeheartedly: "Oh, Mother, someday Richard will be sorry he missed this wonderful gourmet meal." Then, turning to your two-year-old proletarian, say: "Would you like your old standby sandwich?"

Summary

If you expect social graces from a toddler, you are going to be disappointed. A toddler does not yet understand that other people have rights and that every toy in the world doesn't belong to her. But don't worry, within another year or two most children will adopt the manners and graces of their parents.

This is the time to forget about appropriate behavior. Even though you may use the word *share,* don't expect your toddler to understand it and follow through on command.

Parents can learn a lot about how their toddler socializes through playdates. This is a slow, sure way of getting a child to feel comfortable with children her own age. Parents can also help encourage their children, whether they are shy or aggressive, by helping them express their feelings through words and supporting their dramatic play.

Of course, different parents are going to have different reactions when their toddler hits, bites, or refuses to share. It's really important to stop and reflect whether your embarrassment is your issue or whether your toddler is showing normal development that is a bit embarrassing.

▼ ▼ ▼ ▼ ▼ ▼ ▼ ▼ ▼ ▼ ▼ ▼ ▼ ▼ ▼ ▼ ▼ ▼ ▼

CHAPTER 2

Separation

THE KEY ISSUE OF TODDLERHOOD IS SEPARATION. FROM feeding himself to saying good-bye to refusing to walk one step farther, a toddler is constantly working on becoming a separate, independent person. Even his new oratorial skills, which seem to center on the words "no" and "I do it," show that he's striking out on his own.

A baby literally can't tell where her parents end and she begins physically or emotionally. Starting at around the age of one the separation process begins as your child first crawls, then stands on her own two feet, and finally moves out from your sphere of protection.

Separation can be as bittersweet and difficult for parents as it is for toddlers. In the parent groups, mothers and fathers remember how they felt during their own separations from their parents, for example, when leaving home for college, getting married, or moving away. Parents often wonder whether their toddler is having trouble separating because they find it so painful to let go of him. One of my friends, who is now a grandmother, recently remarked,

"From the moment you have your child you spend the rest of your life learning how to separate from him."

No child suddenly wakes up one morning and says, "Wow, this is who I am," but instead defines herself gradually by testing what she can do and how grown-ups react to her budding self. One moment she may say she wants to do everything herself and then a second later she clings to you for dear life, plaintively insisting that Mommy and Daddy do everything for her. This constant swing from dependence to independence occurs because at the same time that a toddler wants to be near her parents she also yearns to explore the world.

Even what seems the smallest request on the part of parents can set off a major power struggle. Power struggles are common with children this age because they are a toddler's way of finding himself. One parent complained that her son was becoming a finicky gourmet all in the name of discovering himself. "He wants his toast buttered, so I butter it, then, of course, he doesn't want it buttered. I take it away and give him another piece. He throws it on the floor and says, 'No toast.' " Dressing can be another opportunity for a toddler to try out her newfound independence. Says one father: "I would give her what I think are her favorite clothes because we are already late for a birthday party. She would then insist on putting on a pink striped shirt, pink plaid pants, and smearing pink lipstick on her lips. I pretend she's not my child when we are on the street."

In order to define who he is, a toddler needs to do things for himself, by himself, and in his own way. The more he does for himself with the understanding support of his parents, the better he'll feel about his own autonomy.

As you go through the ups and downs of your child's attempts at independence, remember that separation really is a celebratory event. By the end of toddlerhood most children settle into their own skins, accepting themselves as independent from you. Also, it may help to keep in mind that you probably won't get all this high drama again until adolescence. By then, you'll be an old pro at identity crises.

This chapter includes wide-ranging advice on what parents should say to a toddler when going out for an evening or heading off for work, what toys can help their child master his feelings about comings and goings, how the process may affect parents, and how parents can meet their toddler's as well as their own needs during this period.

▼ ▼ ▼ ▼ ▼ ▼ ▼ ▼ ▼ ▼ ▼ ▼ ▼ ▼ ▼ ▼ ▼ ▼

What Your Toddler May Act Like During Separation

What you may find your toddler trying out on the way to Who am I? All these ways of behaving are typical and normal.

    1. **Mountain climbing.** You may find her climbing on tables, jumping from slides, testing her physical prowess in space.

Now's the time to put the limit on where your toddler can jump, such as on a home trampoline or climbing gym.

2. Routines can become impossible. Dressing, eating, sleeping may take more time and energy than you ever thought possible. Remember, try not to overwhelm your child with choices.

3. Total unreasonableness seems to overtake him. *No* becomes his favorite word even when he wants to say yes. If you sit in a chair that he suddenly decides is his and don't obey his commands to move within three seconds, he may well throw a passionate tantrum. Remember, pick your battles. Give him the chair, and his interest in owning the throne will disappear faster than if you make a big deal of it.

4. "I want to be a baby." Suddenly your child, who can feed herself and who has been walking since ten months of age, says plaintively to you, "Feed me, carry me." Why not grant your toddler half a wish? Pick her up saying, "You want to be a baby," but then bring her back to her full thirty pounds a few minutes later by putting her on the ground and saying, "Now you are my big girl again."

5. Sleep can become a nightmare. Going to sleep can become exhausting because he now doesn't want to sleep without his parents or to go to sleep in his own bed if he hears you enjoying a quiet adult conversation. Remember, this is the time for your child to learn how to enjoy his own company and fall asleep on his own. It takes experience to learn how to sleep.

6. Parting is not sweet sorrow. Whereas you used to walk out the door knowing that your chosen caretaker would handle your sweet, cooing baby's needs magnificently, it's now like leaving a heartbroken suitor who clings desperately to you for

dear life. It's painful for both of you. It isn't only your baby
who is suffering, it's hard on you, too. Remember the
mantra: "Mommy and Daddy always come back."

▲ ▲ ▲ ▲ ▲ ▲ ▲ ▲ ▲ ▲ ▲ ▲ ▲ ▲ ▲ ▲ ▲ ▲ ▲ ▲

So Long, Farewell

Every child generally has her own style of reacting when her parents
leave her. She may sob hysterically and have a real tantrum; she may
withdraw into a corner, looking down at the floor and barely
answering even the most cheerful, loving voice; she may pull down
every toy from the shelf and hit anyone who dares to look at her
possessions; or she may lie down and go to sleep.

When you return home you'll probably hear from the caregiver
that your child was soon able to enjoy play. The problem is, of
course, that when you walk through the door he very well might
start whining and screaming just to let you know that he's missed
you. After all, whom else can he take it out on? Or you may find
that, much to your delight and surprise, he runs gleefully into your
arms crying "Mommy, Daddy" and then resumes playing with
gusto.

However, because of the intensity of this separation period,
there are going to be days when you return and nothing seems to
have gone right. Your caregiver may report that your child hardly
stopped crying and that the words that usually comfort her, for
example, "Mommy and Daddy always come back," fell on deaf ears.
When your toddler suddenly has a dramatic change in his personality, try to look at the last few days of your life and your child's
life to solve the mystery. Most of the time you'll be able to figure out
why he is out of sorts.

Sometimes a child's difficulty separating has very little to do
with the actual parting. She really could be upset about something
else. Everything affects a child during this time.

Parents have to make an educated guess when their child

suddenly can't stand being away from them. For example, if your independent, bubbly daughter starts sobbing every time you step out of her sight, what is going on? Is the new baby's cuteness winning everyone's heart? Have you been out at night more often? Is she overtired? Is she getting over a cold? Were you preoccupied with phone calls? Were you away over the weekend? Are you and your partner more tense and angry than usual? Says one mother: "I kept thinking about every possible reason. Maybe she didn't like the baby-sitter anymore, maybe she had a bad day in the park. The one thing I didn't think of was that my husband and I weren't getting along. We were incredibly tense and probably the worst thing was that we weren't even admitting our disagreements."

▼ ▼ ▼ ▼ ▼ ▼ ▼ ▼ ▼ ▼ ▼ ▼ ▼ ▼ ▼ ▼ ▼ ▼ ▼

Situations That Can Intensify Separation Difficulties

1. Starting playschool.

2. Toddler, parents, or siblings sick.

3. Parents away on trips.

4. Parents not spending enough time home with child.

5. New caregiver.

6. New baby.

7. Job stress.

8. Parents fighting.

9. Parents depressed.

10. Moving.

11. Divorce.

12. Death.

▲ ▲ ▲ ▲ ▲ ▲ ▲ ▲ ▲ ▲ ▲ ▲ ▲ ▲ ▲ ▲ ▲ ▲ ▲

Making Good-byes More Palatable

Contrary to what common sense tells you, it's been our experience that it isn't a good idea to prepare a toddler way in advance when you are going out, or, for that matter, telling your child too far in advance of any change in your schedule. This just seems to make toddlers more anxious rather than prepared. (Of course, when your child is older you'll prepare him well ahead of time.)

About a half hour before the baby-sitter arrives, try saying very directly: "Dad and I are going out to dinner. Lucy is going to stay with you. We'll be back after you go to sleep. We'll come in and kiss you." In other words, give your explanation clearly, succinctly, and without any guilt.

If possible, have the baby-sitter arrive at least thirty minutes or so early. When parents spend time with the sitter, it helps a toddler feel that the sitter is safe and usually makes the transition from mother and father to caregiver much smoother.

When you are ready to leave, make the good-bye short and sweet. Tell your child where you are going and when you'll be returning. Hours don't mean much to a toddler, so let him know in child time (after his nap, before *Sesame Street*) when you'll be home. "Mommy and Daddy are leaving to go see Grandpa. We'll be back after your nap." At the Toddler Center we have found that it reassures a child to top off the good-bye with the loving mantra, "Mommy and Daddy always come back."

Try not to hesitate when you go out the door even if your child starts to cry. A toddler's anxiety only escalates if her parents seem ambivalent. Good-byes are easier when the parent is decisive and calm. For instance, it doesn't help a toddler when her parents get caught up in the emotional frenzies of good-byes like this: "I'm going now. Let me give you another kiss and hug. I'm not going to cry. I don't want you to cry. Are you going to cry?"

When parents can't accept the fact that their toddler has very passionate feelings about separating, the child often senses their discomfort and acts out more. Says one mother: "My son is the only one in the playgroup who screams every time I leave. I can't help but cringe with embarrassment. Sometimes, even though I know it is horrible, I wish every other child was screaming."

It can be wrenching for loving parents to understand that children are allowed to have a hard time and feel sad emotions. If you smooth over every difficult situation for your child, how will he gain the experience to learn to cope by himself? In order for your child to develop into an autonomous individual, he must at times endure separations from his mother or father.

But no matter how hard it is to face your child's sadness, don't ever sneak out without saying good-bye. It's important for your toddler to trust you, even if it means that by telling her the truth she'll be upset. For instance, if you are going out alone with your spouse for a social evening, don't pretend you are going to work because you feel guilty about enjoying yourself. If you can be honest, it will help your child rely on you throughout her life.

▼ ▼ ▼ ▼ ▼ ▼ ▼ ▼ ▼ ▼ ▼ ▼ ▼ ▼ ▼ ▼ ▼ ▼ ▼

How Parents Know if They Are Having Difficulties Separating

1. Prolonging the good-byes (too many kisses and hugs, too many suggestions on what the child should do, too many "one more story's").

2. Asking their child if she is going to miss them.

3. Providing too many explanations of why they have to leave (in other words, they are feeling guilty).

4. Overly empathic (a little goes a long way).

5. Hesitant about walking out the door. Parents shouldn't take two steps forward and one back, but march firmly onward.

6. Unable to accept that sometimes their child will have a hard time separating.

7. Wondering constantly if their child is able to settle down and able to use his caregiver for comfort.

8. Sneaking out rather than saying a direct farewell.

◆ ◆ ◆ ◆ ◆ ◆ ◆ ◆ ◆ ◆ ◆ ◆ ◆ ◆ ◆ ◆ ◆

Toys That Help in Separation

Some toys and games will not only delight your toddler, but also help her act out her drama of separating from her mother and father.

- ◆ Peekaboo
- ◆ Run away and catch me games
- ◆ Jack-in-the-box
- ◆ Tunnels, bridge, choo choo train
- ◆ Cash registers
- ◆ Pull toys
- ◆ Play phones

These toys and games can help your toddler feel some control over his environment. They all allow him to act out what he is experiencing emotionally, going away and coming back. For example, when he pushes the toy car through the tunnel, he is very often practicing his own comings and goings. Or when the jack-in-the-box disappears and suddenly reappears again, it is a comforting reminder that people go away and return. Your child's repeating these games over and over helps him master his uneasy feelings about separation.

▲ ▲ ▲ ▲ ▲ ▲ ▲ ▲ ▲ ▲ ▲ ▲ ▲ ▲ ▲ ▲ ▲ ▲

Good-byes for the Working Parent

For a working parent every morning can be a special time for your toddler. Maybe you can eat breakfast together or read a very, very, very short story together. I know this isn't always easy when you are tired and rushed, but the little extra attention does pay off for a more relaxed separation.

Telephone your toddler at the same time every day if possible. Even if your toddler remains eerily silent on the other end of the phone, he will feel comforted knowing that you are thinking of him. Keep your phone conversations sweet and brief. You can say something like: "Hi, I'm at work. I'll see you after your bath and will read your favorite story. I know you're going to the park now—have fun. Love you."

Leaving photographs of yourself around the house is always reassuring for a toddler.

Finally, come home when you are expected. You'll not only have a happier child, but a much happier caregiver as well.

How to Help Your Toddler Separate

Set Limits   On the way to independence, a toddler may test just about every rule in his parents' book. "If a toddler is giving you a hard time, it's a good sign," says Dr. J. Lawrence Aber, former director of the Toddler Center and current head of the National Center for Children in Poverty. "Without bumping up against your limits, he wouldn't be able to define himself."

Limits help give your toddler some balance in her difficult world. Without these boundaries a toddler can feel scared and confused about what she can and can't do. Although it can be upsetting to have your child angry at you when you say no, it helps her to figure out where her world stops and her parents' begins.

Sometimes parents believe that their child will become more confident if they give him the freedom to make most of his choices.

But this well-intentioned plan usually backfires. The parent who can rarely say no, who can't stand tears, and who says yes to virtually everything can make her child fearful of his power. If parents are afraid of having someone angry at them, and therefore a separate person, it becomes all the more difficult for a child to feel that he is his own person. He may have trouble saying no to anyone else because he has rarely heard his mother or father say the *N* word. Says one mother: "I feel like I've always been so understanding with my three-year-old. But instead of being confident, she seemed the least assertive in her circle of friends. She was like a slave doing anything her friends do. Now that I'm setting more limits she is beginning to voice her views left and right."

Parents need to decide what they can live with during this period. Dozens of times every day a toddler tries to separate by asserting himself. Yield some power when you can.

- Do you really care whether your child sits in the stroller or walks with you pushing the stroller?

- Do you really care if you have to read the same book to your child every night for a month rather than read the beautiful assortment of books you've so carefully chosen?

- Do you really care if your child walks up the slide backwards?

- Do you really care if your child will wear only clothes that are red and purple?

- Do you really care if your child wants to wear the same shirt five days in a row? (You wash it, of course, every night.)

Give Your Toddler the Chance to Grow Up   Taking an active step in shaping your toddler's world makes her feel happy and competent. It is important to be sensitive to a toddler's need to grow up.

Parents can help their toddler become more independent by giving him the experience of playing by himself. Try getting him used to playing by himself in his bed or room. When he wakes up in the morning, don't rush in at the first squeak. Give him some time to talk to his stuffed animals or to sing a song. When he's busy directing his puppets, don't feel that you have to run in and become a star actor. Instead of investing in an antique toy chest that requires the strength of a weight lifter to open, set up his toys on low shelves so he can pick and choose himself.

Playing alone is not a punishment. When your toddler is happily playing next to you, make yourself available but not overly accommodating. For instance, keep yourself mildly preoccupied by reading a newspaper. But when you do play with your toddler, be there for her. If she has the sneaking suspicion that her parent's mind is elsewhere she'll only cling and demand more. A toddler will rarely want to play alone if she doesn't get the attention she needs when she is with her parents.

The more a toddler knows about his routines and is allowed to participate, the more he'll be able to do things by himself. Put a step by the sink so that he can wash his hands. During bath time let him have his own washcloth while you wash him down. Even allow your toddler to brush his teeth by himself, though you will probably want to have a go the second time around. Include finger foods at meals so that he can feed himself. Remember, you have to count on every routine taking twice as long once your toddler is involved.

When Parents Push Their Toddler Too Hard to Be Independent

Just as some parents overdo keeping their child tied to their apron strings, many parents push their toddler to grow up too quickly. You may know that it's good for your child to be separate, and therefore exaggerate a good thing.

You may put your child in too many playgroups, push him to use a fork before he is physically able, or leave her alone at a playdate or a birthday party before she is emotionally ready.

Remember, a toddler does not separate any faster if parents push. In fact, she could become less independent if her parents don't respond and accept her needs.

It can be hard for parents not to be angry or embarrassed when their child seems to be the only one who rarely ventures more than an inch away. You may feel like saying: "Look, Melanie doesn't need her mommy, nor do Tom, Becca, or any of your friends. Why are you being so clingy?" But parents help their toddler get more comfortable by articulating and accepting his feelings. For example: "It can be pretty scary at a party with all these people, but I bet you can have some fun. Let's walk over to that table with all the crayons."

If there is a new sibling, expect double trouble. A toddler with a new brother or sister is going to need an extra dose of attention and empathy to deal with the separation phase.

What Separation May Trigger for a Parent

Separation can be one of the most emotionally laden issues for a parent. But as I've mentioned before, how you act and feel during this period makes a tremendous difference in how your child separates from you.

It is normal for parents to feel torn. No parents want their toddler to remain a baby in need of constant attention, but to help her become independent can be very difficult. Your own past experience with separating from your loved ones can call forth many unsettling thoughts and emotions that are hard to face.

When parents are very independent or overly dependent, separation can bring up difficulties in setting limits, expressing anger, and saying good-bye. However, if you can be straightforward and recognize what your young child evokes in you, this can be a rewarding time for you to work out issues.

For instance, did you come from a family where there was a forced separation either through death or divorce? Did you come from a family where it was taboo to be tearful and show sadness when your mother and father were going out for the evening? Did you come from a family where limits were rarely set and it was hard to differentiate your thoughts from those of anyone else in the family? Did you basically feel miserable when you had to separate from your own parents for school, camp, or sleep-over dates? How were you treated when you tried to assert your own budding independence? Were you taken to task in a shameful, humiliating way, or were you treated with general respect even when you had gone a bit too far? Was it the family style to have a hard time separating or were your parents direct and calm when they said good-bye?

Recollecting their own past can help parents see themselves more honestly during their toddler's separation. However, if the separation period is extremely stressful, by all means consider some outside help to make this time better for you and your child.

How to Get What You Want and Meet Your Toddler's Needs

What prevents parents from having a good time with their toddler? If you are doing a lot of yelling and punishing and feeling frustrated, it may be that you and your toddler are at cross-purposes. Remember that life doesn't have to be like this. Yes, this can be a tough age, but you and your toddler can still enjoy each other. The rule of thumb is that when you recognize a behavior in your child that upsets, embarrasses, or angers you, you need to try to figure out what this behavior is telling you and then try to meet your toddler's needs and yours at the same time.

A lot of parents may say: Why should I accommodate him? Shouldn't he learn to listen to me? My answer is: Of course, your toddler needs to accommodate you, but it will take some time. Right now your understanding of his needs will pay off not only in a happier relationship but with a more secure child. A toddler is not deliberately misbehaving. His outrageous antics are his only way of figuring out who he is. This is the time to put yourself in your toddler's shoes, because he certainly isn't yet able to put himself in yours.

Just think how validated and empowered adults can feel when someone reports in a nonjudgmental way on their mood. "Boy, you really have had a lousy day. It must have been hard when your toddler had six tantrums at your mother-in-law's house." So imagine the relief that a toddler with a limited vocabulary and understanding of her emotions can feel when someone describes in simple words what she is doing and feeling. Parents help their toddler separate by distinguishing her feelings from theirs and others'.

For example, when your toddler is driving you crazy by whining or yelling you might say, "Stop whining or I won't listen to anything you say," but you'll only lose with this order. He may stop whining with threats, but in the long run, which may be ten minutes from now, he'll start whining again because you haven't focused on why he's whining. How about saying: "I know you don't like me to be on the phone and you need me now. As soon as I finish this phone call I'll be with you."

In order to tolerate the insistence of a toddler who wants everything *now*, it makes such a difference first to understand what he is feeling and then to address his needs. By understanding what a toddler is really expressing, parents often seem to feel less put upon and angry. However, if you feel that it is very hard to be empathic, go back to your past once more. For instance, how pleased were your parents when you stood up for what you wanted? How much slack did they give you, or was the household rigid with rules?

▼ ▼ ▼ ▼ ▼ ▼ ▼ ▼ ▼ ▼ ▼ ▼ ▼ ▼ ▼ ▼ ▼ ▼

Normal Separation Behavior and How to Respond

1. **Throwing a temper tantrum.** (Accept it. Some parents hold the child, others let the tantrum kick itself out.) "I see you're

angry. It's okay to be angry. I won't let you hurt yourself or me. When you are finished crying you can tell me what happened."

2. Clinging. "Sometimes it's very hard for you to let Mommy go. Let's you and I have a hug." (By the way, as long as clinging makes a parent angry it probably won't stop.)

3. Ignoring the parent when he or she leaves. "I see you can't say good-bye. It's okay to feel sad. I love you and I always come back."

4. Unexpectedly withdrawing. Sit near the withdrawn child and say: "Sometimes people get sad when mommies and daddies leave. It's okay to be sad. You can tell me when you are sad. I'm just going to sit next to you now and read a story."

5. Exhibiting mood swings. "Today you really seem to feel beside yourself. I'm going to sit down near you. When you're ready I'm going to give you a hug."

6. Acting very aggressive. "I see you want to make Laura cry. I can't let you hurt anyone and nobody will hurt you. It's okay to be angry because Mommy and Daddy are leaving."

7. Crying at the slightest provocation. Put your healing arms around her and say: "You seem very sad today with lots of tears. Let me hold you for a minute and give you some hugs."

8. Being very active physically. "Wow, you really are exploring and going all over the place."

9. Using self-assertive language, such as "Go away," or "I do it." "That's right, you can do it yourself."

▲ ▲ ▲ ▲ ▲ ▲ ▲ ▲ ▲ ▲ ▲ ▲ ▲ ▲ ▲ ▲ ▲ ▲ ▲ ▲

▼ ▼ ▼ ▼ ▼ ▼ ▼ ▼ ▼ ▼ ▼ ▼ ▼ ▼ ▼ ▼ ▼ ▼ ▼

Common Concerns

Q: Should I be bribing my daughter with candy and new toys when I leave her with the baby-sitter?

You are teaching your daughter how to comfort herself with material goods and food rather than letting her have a few minutes of discomfort so that she can learn how to get over her sadness. Even though it is easier to leave a happy toddler, I would try to keep these material bribes to a minimum. Every child is entitled to her emotions. Let her feel an honest sadness or anger when you leave. At the same time, try comforting her with your own words by saying something like: "I'll be back after your bath. Meanwhile, Lola will take good care of you."

Q: My son begs me to put him to sleep before I go out at night. Should I try to keep him up?

Your son has developed his own coping mechanisms to deal with separation. A lot of children would rather go to sleep than have a babysitter put them to sleep. I see nothing wrong with putting your son to sleep as long as you are honest about going out. Try saying something like: "Mommy and Daddy are going to the movies. Janet is here to take care of you. Let me tuck you in."

Q: Ever since the baby was born my toddler won't go into a room by herself, let alone let me out the door.

It takes time for a toddler to get used to a new sibling. After the birth of a baby every child needs more parental involvement, just, of course, when you are overwhelmed and overworked. This clingy behavior will take care of itself as your toddler gets used to her new sibling. But until then you can expect her to be less independent.

If she needs you to walk into a room with her, do it. It's important to give her what she needs. Try saying something like: "I know you really want to be alone with us. Mommy and Daddy will always be here for you."

Q: I don't work, and I come and go from my house a lot during the day. I go to my computer class and come home. Then maybe I go out for a lunch date. Later on I often go out again on errands. Are all these good-byes hard for my son?

To the child being left, whether his mother or father works is not important. But if you are coming in and out constantly it can make your child upset, even with a great baby-sitter. Do you give your child time to feel you are there for him, even if it's for a short period? If you come and go in a harried state or sneak in and out, it will affect your toddler. I recommend that you build into your comings and goings enough time to really connect. Try spending at least forty-five minutes with your toddler before you go out again. But remember that a satisfied parent is what makes a child happy.

Q: When do I need to spend more time with my child?

A child needs more individual time with her mother and father whenever there are changes in her routine, such as a new baby-sitter, a new playgroup, a new sibling, returning home from a vacation, or after being sick. Your child will also need to see you more when there is a crisis in the family.

Of course, if you have been home much less than usual lately, your toddler will also need more of you.

Q: My child used to have no trouble separating, but suddenly he seems to be finding it very difficult.

For every two steps forward there is often one step back. Anything can trigger separation difficulty. You need to figure out if there have been any recent changes that are affecting his life. Has your family just returned from vacation and started up their busy lives once again, leaving less time for your toddler?

Q: I work all week. My child seems used to these separations but goes crazy when I go out on the weekend.

You probably feel a difference when you go to work, which is a necessity, and when you go out for pleasure (which is also a necessity). You may feel guilty leaving your toddler to do something for yourself. But remember, parents need to have their own life in order to be giving. If you go out Saturday night, be sure to give your child some concentrated time during the day.

Q: My child watches television when I leave for work every morning. She doesn't even come out to say hello to the baby-sitter.

It sounds as though you are imagining that your child sits in the room all day alone watching television. I would tell the baby-sitter your concerns. You might need her to reassure you that one minute after you have left she and your daughter are reading stories together. You also might find it easier if your baby-sitter watches TV with your child when you leave. Incidentally, I see nothing wrong with your child watching her favorite program when you are departing for work. Just make certain that you say good-bye.

Summary

Separation is the most important developmental stage of toddlerhood. This is the time when your toddler gets a sense of independence from his mother and father. Separation and individuation are the milestones that every toddler must achieve on the way to growing from a baby to a preschooler.

Separation affects all areas of a toddler's life, from sleeping to eating to play. But it isn't an easy period. Your toddler may become very negative and mercurial, testing out who she is against you. In other words, it can be a giant power struggle.

If you have had trouble in your own life with defining your boundaries from those of your parents, then this will give you a second chance to redo those sticky issues. A toddler always seems to uncover her parents' Achilles' heels as well as pour salt on their wounds. If you find it difficult to say good-bye to her, she may keep you up all night. Would you rather stay home than face your toddler's tears and screams? Then I assure you she will end up an award-winning actor.

Every child goes through separation. The whole family will have an easier time if routines are established and followed, firm limits are set, and point-blank "No's" are used sparingly. Even saying good-bye when you are going off to work or a movie can be easier for your toddler if you are calm and decisive.

The process, however difficult, really is a joyful event. After all, your toddler is coming into his own for the first time.

▼ ▼ ▼ ▼ ▼ ▼ ▼ ▼ ▼ ▼ ▼ ▼ ▼ ▼ ▼ ▼ ▼ ▼

CHAPTER 3

Setting Limits

SK ANY PARENT—THE ONE ISSUE THAT NEVER GOES away is setting limits. Should we say no, should we say yes, or should we just keep quiet? Limit setting is difficult because, just as we want to build our child's budding self-esteem, so we also want a child we can live with. Being firm with a toddler is about the hardest parenting task around. This little explorer has just pulled himself out of the warm cocoon of babyhood and is trying to get his own sense of belonging. In fact, he may spend all his waking hours testing out how much power he has. "No," "I want that," "That's mine," and screaming tantrums are, after all, how two-year-olds get their bad reputations.

But tough and fearless as a toddler can seem, she is also very scared of all this new independence. A two-year-old needs boundaries in order to feel secure and discover herself. Without limits a toddler seems to feel that the world is a very scary place over which she has no control.

Life can be very tricky when it comes to laying down the law for a toddler. It's easy to be clear about the obvious rules. For instance, you probably don't negotiate with your child about whether he has to go to the pediatrician, just as you don't negotiate about his crossing the street without a grown-up, touching a strange dog, or sitting in the car seat.

However, beyond these basic rules, which deal mostly with safety, there are probably dozens of times during the day when you have to decide whether to say yes or no. My basic philosophy is to keep nos to a minimum and give your toddler power over anything that is not worth your energy to fight about. For example, do you really care if he wears a striped shirt with plaid pants? Aesthetically, it may blind and embarrass you. But it does enable him to feel that he has some choice in his little universe. Give in. You don't want to squash his curiosity and spontaneity as he explores the world.

I hear many parents say that they don't make their homes childproof because they want their child to learn to obey. If you follow this course you'll be saying "No" all day long and in a constant battle. A toddler learns through her senses. She touches, tastes, pulls, takes apart, disconnects, and puts things together in her own fashion. At the Toddler Center the room is set up so that the children can explore safely without adults constantly trailing them. Plugs are in outlets, cleaning fluids are stored in unreachable closets, and doors are locked.

Setting Limits at Your Toddler's Level

There are many factors to consider when you are setting limits. You want to focus on where your child is rather than where you think he should be. Here are some things to keep in mind:

1. He acts out of bounds not because he is purposely out to drive you crazy, but to establish his independence. Therefore, be a benevolent dictator; when you set rules, remember to give him his share of power.

2. She is no longer a baby, but at the same time she is not yet a full-fledged child. Expect her to throw her two-year-old tantrums when you set down the law.

3. His memory is very short, which may mean that he really doesn't remember when you say, "I've told you almost every day for a month not to paint on the wall."

4. She wants everything now. Try negotiating, substituting, and delaying gratification in small doses. "I know you want to go to the park. As soon as I put these dishes away we're off." Or, "Oh, I see you really want that candy bar. How about having a cracker and helping me get your stroller to go outside?"

5. He doesn't have a clear sense of right and wrong. His mother and father still are his conscience. The farther he is from you physically, the more likely he is to forget everything you told him about what is good and bad.

6. She seems to be learning words so quickly that you may think she understands everything. But become the guest lecturer from Harvard, giving complicated explanations for every rule, and you'll lose her. Don't say, "You must wash your hands because they are full of bacteria and you could get an infectious disease that would be hard to cure with the strongest antibiotics," when "Let's wash our hands" will do the trick.

7. He often doesn't understand the difference between real and pretend. He may eat play-dough cookies as if they really were cookie batter.

8. Some battles you can't avoid, some you can. She is physically able to get around and over almost everything. Remove the fragile crystal bowls and lock up dangerous liquids unless you want to be a guard all day.

Punishments: Spanking, Time-out, or No Ice Cream for a Week?

It is very hard for the parent of a toddler to know how to handle her outbursts. At times you may feel like screaming yourself, running out the door and passing your toddler to the first adult who is willing to take her off your hands, or giving her an old-fashioned spanking.

It's unbelievable how such a tiny person can get parents to feel so out of control. Your initial reaction might very well be to spank. However, a good whack (as almost every child development book now advises), while it may relieve your anger, will only teach your child that big people hit. Even worse, spanking a child can diminish his self-respect and self-esteem. Remember that the purpose of disciplining a child is to teach him how to deal with his intolerable feelings in a reasonable way.

So what can you do to get your toddler back to acting reasonable again? Many parents are surprised that I recommend giving a time-out to such young children. But I've seen that a few minutes alone in a room or sitting in a chair can help a toddler pull himself back together. Time-out gives parents and child an immediate break from each other. It sets a boundary in the here and now.

In a firm voice, say something like: "Uncivilized behavior isn't acceptable in our house. Go sit in your room until you feel you can behave." Big words such as *uncivilized* instantly impress a toddler, not because he can understand them or look them up in the dictionary, but because they show him that you mean business. Punishments don't work when a mother or father seems hesitant, apologetic, or meek.

There's no reason to shut the door. You want your child to feel free to come out when she is ready (another way of giving her some power over the situation), which probably will be soon. Even if she should emerge still on the verge of a tantrum, your goal has been accomplished. The situation has been defused. It's important to show your child that even though you punished her you still love her. How about saying: "I see you did go into your room. But it is hard for you to stay there now. Do you need me to hold and calm you?"

It is very tempting to resort to bribery—who among us hasn't? Witholding special treats (usually sweets) from a toddler or offering something (also usually sweets) can command instant obedience. "If you don't stop spilling that paint you won't have dessert for a week," or "If you stop throwing your toys off the shelves we'll go to the ice cream store."

But long term, bribery just doesn't work. Your toddler will come to expect a prize for all his behavior. You want him to set his own inner controls. Unlike toilet training, which can take a few weeks, learning how to be in control of emotions and actions is a lifelong process for everybody. Losing control becomes exaggerated at a toddler's age because he constantly needs to check his power against everyone else.

One other piece of advice that you may not hear very often: You and your partner each have a different relationship with your child. You can feel constantly undermined if you think that you both need to take a similiar stance on everything. It's not a big deal if your two-year-old knows that his father lets him push the grocery cart, while his mother makes him sit in it. Or that Mommy will give him three cookies for a snack, whereas Daddy will only give him two. After all, your toddler is getting the experience of being with different people.

But when it comes to big issues about which you feel very strongly, such as holding an adult's hand when crossing the street, there should be one rule. Talk with your partner about what and why certain issues are important to you and what your joint position should be.

When you do say no to your toddler, make sure your partner backs you up. Remember, children at this age are prone to check their power against everyone. If he doesn't like what he hears from one parent, he'll dash off hopefully to the other.

▼ ▼ ▼ ▼ ▼ ▼ ▼ ▼ ▼ ▼ ▼ ▼ ▼ ▼ ▼ ▼ ▼
Instead of Saying No

When you set limits, you are trying to get your toddler to be a little less frustrated and at the same time help his self-esteem to flourish. Too many point-blank "No's" will dampen his curiosity. He may very well turn you off and even think you don't like him.

Try using "No" as a powerful weapon only when you really need it, when he could hurt himself or others. The other countless

times you set boundaries, try using some of the softer phrases that
follow. You won't come down like a ton of bricks, but at the same
time you won't be giving in.

> 1. "I wish I could let you throw all the sand out of the
> sandbox. But how about pouring it in this bucket?" (You are
> acknowledging your child's wish, but not acting on it. Old-
> fashioned substitution really does work.)
>
> 2. "I understand that you want to eat all the cookies in the
> world." (Empathizing can melt anyone.)
>
> 3. "I've never seen anyone pour milk on pizza before!" (A
> sense of humor goes a long way with a toddler.)
>
> 4. "Oh, I see you want to paint. Right now we are going to
> put this play dough away. Then in a few minutes we'll bring
> out the easel." (Use delayed gratification in small doses.)

▲ ▲ ▲ ▲ ▲ ▲ ▲ ▲ ▲ ▲ ▲ ▲ ▲ ▲ ▲ ▲ ▲ ▲ ▲ ▲

When It Can Be Hard for Parents to Set Limits

If you feel that you have to be liked all the time by everybody, that
you need to be a friend to your child every hour of every day, that it
is almost always your fault when he acts out, or if you have trouble
getting angry, then it could be tough for you to set limits. Says one
mother: "I feel like every time I say no to my toddler it's such a huge
decision. I first have to talk it over with myself: 'Should I say no?
Should I set a limit? Should I ignore her? Does it make sense?'
Setting limits is so hard because I rarely can spontaneously just say
'no.' In fact, I often don't even realize that I am angry with my
daughter until much later. I always seem to find excuses to justify
her behavior."

For those of you who find it hard to recognize angry feelings, it
often helps to give yourself permission to react. When you feel even
the slightest twinge of being upset, try to look inside at how you

feel. Then let your toddler know. For example: "It makes me angry when I see all those broken eggs on the floor. Eggs are for eating, not playing. Come on, let's clean them up."

On the other hand, if you are a person who often feels angry, who is a perfectionist down to the tiniest detail, and who perhaps even enjoys having people a little fearful of you, then you also may have a hard time with limits. You can't stop setting them. Don't repeat the problems given to you by your parents. One father explains: "My parents always had strict, unbendable limits. I could never buy anything but navy shoes, and I always had to go to sleep at exactly eight o'clock every night until I was ten. So now I expect my son to follow my instructions exactly. Underneath it all I feel that if I don't set strict limits about almost everything, he really will go out of control. What's funny is that I didn't like all these limits when I was young, but I guess I am on automatic."

Both these parenting styles have the same effect on a toddler. He won't feel as safe and well taken care of as a child who is given reasonable limits that respect the fact that he's only two and is just learning about his world.

Shame

Starting at around two years of age a toddler feels a new emotion: shame. Before this age most children don't seem to care very much if they aren't capable of living up to someone else's performance. But once a child begins to incorporate outside standards, she can suddenly feel inadequate. Says one father: "I always drew a picture of our house for our son, saying, 'You can do this too.' Before he was two, he would just happily scribble his version of the house. But at two-and-a-half, he would throw a tantrum and say, 'Oh, no, I can't draw like you!' "

While being able to feel a sense of shame is a sign that your toddler is finally becoming civilized and beginning to know what standards you are setting for him, I don't recommend shaming your child.

How many of us parents can still remember hearing, "I'm surprised you did that. You are suppose to be a big girl," "Only babies cry. Look at those crocodile tears," or "You're being disgusting. Don't put your thumb in your mouth"?

It is hard to trust and feel confident if you are often humiliated. And your toddler won't miss out on the opportunity to experience shame. Every day he is exposed to the world's standards and his inability to live up to them.

When Parents Feel Out of Control

You may feel that the day is never going to end, that you can't deal with another scene from your toddler. If you had a hard day at work with your boss breathing down your neck, you may come home and want to act like the baby, cranky, tired, in need of nurturing.

Since most of us have a limited amount of patience, it can be easy to lose it when our toddler goes into her typical toddler routine of saying "No!" and being totally unreasonable and excessive. You can feel as if she is out to get you.

Don't consider yourself a terrible parent if you are so angry at your toddler that your insides are screaming. This happens to all of us.

But if you really do blow up and let it all out, your child can feel scared and humiliated. Constant screaming can be as devastating for a toddler as physical abuse.

Once you get hold of yourself (the quicker, the better), try apologizing. "I'm sorry I screamed at you. I should not have screamed at you. I love you." Then how about figuring out why you are so angry that you feel pushed to the limit? Is it really your toddler, or is something else in your life bothering you? Are you feeling frustrated on the job or at home? If you are angry at your partner, why not face him or her directly. Says one father: "When my wife and I were having bad marital problems, my fuse was very short with my daughter. Once we started seeing a counselor and talked things out, I found myself a lot less frustrated and warmer toward my daughter."

Or, once again, you could be tripped up by your past history. Reports one mother: "When I fought with my two-year-old daughter I think I was reliving the horrible competition and fights I had with my younger sister. My parents were also always yelling at me."

But it is never too late to learn control for your sake and for the sake of your toddler. When you feel as though you are about to lose it, get out of the situation. Try going into the bathroom, getting a drink of water, counting to ten, or turning on soothing music.

Over the years I've seen how helpful parent groups can be. Mothers and fathers find relief in talking to each other, getting out feelings they can't express to almost anyone else. However, if you feel that your getting out of control is becoming uncontrollable, speak to a mental health professional.

▼ ▼ ▼ ▼ ▼ ▼ ▼ ▼ ▼ ▼ ▼ ▼ ▼ ▼ ▼ ▼ ▼ ▼

How to Talk and Set Limits

1. State your feelings. "I don't like it when you throw the Cheerios on the floor."

2. Don't blame the doer. Instead of "You are so messy and clumsy," try saying, "I see you spilled your Cheerios. I'll help you clean them up."

3. Talk about the actions. "The rule here is that we don't spill Cheerios, we eat them."

4. Be positive. Don't ask questions that can be answered with a "No." Try "Let's clean up," rather than "Do you want to clean up?" (By the way, your toddler has done an exemplary cleaning job if she manages to put two Cheerios in the dustpan!)

▲ ▲ ▲ ▲ ▲ ▲ ▲ ▲ ▲ ▲ ▲ ▲ ▲ ▲ ▲ ▲ ▲ ▲

What It Means When Your Child Acts Up

There are moments during the day when your toddler is going to give you strong signals that she really needs you. If you've been away at work all day or on a trip, she may burst into tears at the sight of you coming through the door. If you've been constantly carrying dishes of ice cream to an older brother who is sick in bed, or cuddling a colicky newborn, your toddler may throw herself on the floor and have a full-blown tantrum.

Mothers and fathers are the most meaningful people in a child's life. Your toddler is brimming with feeling for you. After all, she really doesn't understand why you left her for a job or why you pay so much attention to a sick brother. She needs you to sit down and hold her.

Tiredness and frustration can also set your toddler off. Is he having a tantrum because he missed his nap? Let him have some quiet time. Is she crying because the puzzles are too hard? Try removing the puzzles and providing different, age-appropriate toys. Is he throwing himself on the floor because you won't let him eat a box of cookies? Give him a cracker for each hand.

Summary

Setting limits for a toddler can be one of the most difficult parenting jobs around. After all, your little explorer may be spending all her waking hours testing how much power she has. Children need boundaries to feel secure and discover themselves.

But life can be very tricky when it comes to laying down the law for a toddler. It's easy to be clear about the obvious rules, for instance, when it comes to his health or safety. But it's the dozens of other times during the day when parents could go either way with a yes or no that can be very confusing. Again, keep point-blank "No's" to a minimum.

Parents who feel they have to be liked or who need to be in control all the time may have difficulty setting reasonable limits. Look to yourself if this issue is particularly frustrating for you. It is important to meet your needs as well as your toddler's when you set limits.

▼ ▼ ▼ ▼ ▼ ▼ ▼ ▼ ▼ ▼ ▼ ▼ ▼ ▼ ▼ ▼ ▼ ▼

CHAPTER 4

Temper Tantrums

CAN THINK OF HARDLY A TODDLER WHO HASN'T HAD HIS fair share of full-blown temper tantrums. While it can be scary and embarrassing for parents to watch their child flail his arms, scream, hit the floor, and even hold his breath to the point of turning blue, tantrums are normal behavior when your two- or three-year-old becomes frustrated.

Why does a toddler have tantrums? She often can't communicate what she needs or is feeling. She certainly doesn't like the word *no*. She gets angry at herself for her lack of physical coordination. But most of all, in the course of discovering who she is, she checks out what power she has versus her parents and, for that matter, the rest of the world.

Anything can set a tantrum off. You could have placed her toys differently on the shelves. Maybe he wasn't allowed to eat his cereal on Grandma's sofa, or he was so overtired that he had to let off some steam. Maybe she couldn't pull on her socks or build a tower without the blocks falling down.

Sometimes parents can head off tantrums if they have a sense of what throws their child into a tizzy. Assess the situation and see what you can do to relieve the pressure. For instance, if you know your toddler loves lollipops, don't leave them in open view. If a puzzle is too difficult for him, substitute one that's easier and put the harder one away until a later time. Or, if you know that she's tired after playgroup, that is not the time to take her on a visit to the supermarket.

▼ ▼ ▼ ▼ ▼ ▼ ▼ ▼ ▼ ▼ ▼ ▼ ▼ ▼ ▼ ▼ ▼ ▼ ▼

What Causes Tantrums: Everything from . . .

1. Not getting what she wants immediately.

2. Encountering parental expectations that are much too high for a toddler.

3. Being overscheduled.

4. Encountering new stresses, such as a new caregiver, playgroup, or sibling.

5. Lacking the communication skills necessary to recognize and label her feelings.

6. Being overtired.

7. Getting sick.

8. Being hungry.

9. Being unable to express his feelings through his own play.

10. Experiencing frustration over her lack of coordination.

11. In other words, LIFE.

▲ ▲ ▲ ▲ ▲ ▲ ▲ ▲ ▲ ▲ ▲ ▲ ▲ ▲ ▲ ▲ ▲ ▲ ▲

"No time for ball, Daddy. I've got daycare til noon, gym class at 2,
a playdate at 4, and a temper tantrum scheduled for 7:30."

But once the tantrum starts, there isn't much you can do because your toddler really is incapable of restraining himself. His anger literally sends him out of control. The most important thing is to stay calm. Reasoning with a frantic toddler or trying to stop a tantrum rarely works. It doesn't help to say, "If you don't stop screaming I won't buy you an ice cream cone," "This is no way to behave. No! No! No!" or "I'll leave you in the street if this behavior doesn't stop immediately." Your child has worked herself up to such a frenzy that she can barely hear you, let alone listen. She'll get over her anger much more quickly if you allow her to express her feelings. Believe it or not, children are scared of the intensity of their outbursts.

The best way we've found to deal with a tantrum is just not to react. Don't have a tantrum yourself! Don't punish, don't reward, and don't placate! But also, don't leave the room, because it may make your toddler feel that his anger is frightening you away. Just sit quietly and calmly next to him.

It's important for parents to protect a toddler during her tantrums. If she destroys things or hurts herself she'll become even more frightened of her strong emotions because her parents haven't been able to protect her from her rage. If your child starts to hurt herself you may have to hold her. But since this restraining action can escalate her anger, I'd recommend first removing all obstacles and then sitting quietly next to her.

Some parents try to bribe their children into a good mood. Says one mother: "The minute I hear the screams start I begin my present list. If you stop crying we'll go to the park. I'll buy you an ice cream. Maybe I'll even buy you a special toy." This cajoling may work in the moment to stop the tantrum, but in the long run rewards will only perpetuate the behavior. The tantrums may become endless.

▼ ▼ ▼ ▼ ▼ ▼ ▼ ▼ ▼ ▼ ▼ ▼ ▼ ▼ ▼ ▼ ▼ ▼

Don'ts for Parents
When Their Toddler Is Having a Tantrum

1. Don't punish.

2. Don't reward.

3. Don't bribe.

4. Don't placate.

5. Don't leave the room.

6. Don't have a tantrum yourself.

▲ ▲ ▲ ▲ ▲ ▲ ▲ ▲ ▲ ▲ ▲ ▲ ▲ ▲ ▲ ▲ ▲ ▲

It can be nerve-racking to watch someone who is out of control. As a parent you may feel it's your job to get your toddler back in control. But remember that your child is blinded by fury and in a little while the tornado will subside. Once your toddler calms down, explain in short sentences why he gets angry. "You really got mad when Mommy said it was time to put the crayons away. It's okay to be angry; next time you can tell me this. You can say, 'Mommy, I get mad when you tell me to put the crayons away.'

Mommy will listen to you. And you know I love you even when you are angry at me."

When parents articulate and label their toddler's feeling it helps a child to recognize and accept her emotions. You are teaching her how to communicate her feelings without resorting to tantrums. As your child gets older, probably four or five years old, it is a good idea to ask the question, "What made you angry?" If your child understands why he gets angry, he can share and assert himself, making him feel more self-assured.

However, if it seems that your child is constantly having tantrums it could be a sign that something is more stressful for her than it should be. It's important to think about why she may be going through such a difficult period. Maybe you are saying no too often instead of giving her some choices. For instance, do you really care if she brushes her teeth before or after she is in her pajamas?

One father recounts: "When we went to her friends' houses my daughter would have a tantrum if she couldn't have all the toys she wanted. When we crossed the street, she would have a tantrum if the light was red. When we went into the grocery store, I could count on her grabbing bags of cookies and screaming. Anything seemed to set her off. I began to feel furious at her. I couldn't stand to be with her."

Once this father was able to calm down, he realized what might be setting his daughter off. "We had just had a baby. My wife and I were so tired that rather than negotiate and empathize with her, we were just saying no constantly. It all was obviously backfiring."

Temper tantrums do eventually subside as your child becomes more verbal about his feelings and more able to delay gratification and act out his feelings through play. The height of negativity usually ends by around age three or three and a half.

▼ ▼ ▼ ▼ ▼ ▼ ▼ ▼ ▼ ▼ ▼ ▼ ▼ ▼ ▼ ▼ ▼ ▼ ▼ ▼

Common Concerns

Q: Sometimes in the middle of my son's tantrum I realize that I should have given into a request.

This happens to all of us. We reconsider our situation. However, better not to have your child feel you are rewarding a tantrum by giving in. Next time you can let your toddler eat that extra cookie.

Q: My child always seems to have tantrums in the supermarket.

The supermarket is almost a cliché in talking about tantrums with children. What toddler doesn't become tempted by all the goodies? In a public place it is very difficult not to feel embarrassed and angry during a tantrum. However, the main idea for the parent is not to give in or to punish the child for his wrath. According to your own threshold, either leave the store immediately or bite the bullet and continue shopping.

As an advocate for parents, I always thought that in addition to the ten-item express lines there should be a "temper tantrum lane" for parents of young children.

Q: I can't deal with my daughter's anger and often leave the room during her tantrums. Is this bad?

Tantrums can really be horrible for a parent. However, if your toddler is having one because she's angry, scared, or frustrated, she may feel abandoned and convinced that her feelings aren't acceptable if she can drive you away. Try understanding that she isn't having a tantrum on purpose and needs you for comfort after the storm passes.

Q: My toddler always seems to have a tantrum just when I want her to behave, for instance, at my in-laws' house.

As far as the tantrum goes, don't reward or punish because of it. What's important is for you to figure out why she is having the tantrum. Is there too much pressure for her to behave? Do you feel anxious before you go to your in-laws'? If it is your anxiety that's putting pressure on your toddler, figure out a way for you to become more relaxed. It may also help to prepare your toddler in advance for the routine at her grandparents' house.

Q: I really feel my child has to learn how to control himself. I take away privileges, like ice cream or television, when he has tantrums.

Although it may feel as though your child is intentionally having a tantrum, he really can't control himself. He is as fearful of what he's doing as you may be. Therefore, punishing him just reinforces his feelings of being out of control. Remember that he has a right to his feelings and you don't want to punish him for having strong ones.

Q: My toddler often seems to have tantrums when I am tired and have a hard time making a decision about whether to give in to his pleas for another toy, another ice cream.

When parents are indecisive and waffle, you can be sure that a toddler will home in on the ambivalence and have a tantrum to clinch the deal. Let's face it, toddlers have their own built-in antennae that pick up on parents' emotional wavelengths.

Summary

As a parent you may feel that it's your job to get your toddler back in control, but temper tantrums are part of the life of every toddler. A tantrum occurs when a child is frustrated. He lacks the communication skills to express his feelings. Frustration escalates to anger and then becomes out of control.

That said, you may be able to head off a tantrum if you know what situations drive your toddler crazy. But once a tantrum starts, it's impossible to reason with this impassioned person. Remove all dangerous and fragile obstacles as she hurls herself on the floor, and protect her from injury to herself. Patiently sit next to her and let the tantrum run its course. Don't reward, don't punish, don't have a tantrum yourself. Let your child have her feelings.

After the tantrum has subsided and you are both feeling more in control, talk about how he can express himself with words. Think about how you can play act with him to get out his feelings. Use his toys and reenact a similar situation: "The mommy elephant gets the baby elephant really angry when she says no to more television."

▼ ▼ ▼ ▼ ▼ ▼ ▼ ▼ ▼ ▼ ▼ ▼ ▼ ▼ ▼ ▼ ▼ ▼ ▼ ▼

Eating

ATING IS RIGHT AT THE TOP OF MANY PARENTS' WORRY list. I hear parents say over and over that their toddler doesn't eat enough, eats too much, hates vegetables, loves sugar, won't stay seated at meals, fights every bite.

If you think back to babyhood, it's no wonder feeding stirs up so much emotion. Starting at birth, every mouthful of food a newborn takes becomes linked to love and nurturing. How much a baby eats at a 2 A.M. feeding can make us feel we are good or bad parents. A baby's intake is a major measure of how she is adjusting to life. It is also a major conversation piece when anyone asks how the baby is doing.

Unfortunately, it seems to me that most children develop eating problems precisely because parents get too involved. Feeding often becomes a power struggle between the parents wanting to control how much their child eats and the toddler wanting to take charge of her own appetite. I believe that a parent's power should simply be to choose and serve the food; a child's power should be to decide whether to eat or not.

In my parent groups we talk about what to do when mothers and fathers find themselves involved in controlling how much their toddler eats through such tactics as "Here comes the choo choo train into the tunnel," "No *Sesame Street* unless you clean that plate," or "I'll buy you an ice cream cone if you eat your broccoli."

It really is possible to get out of this power struggle. For example, let's say you are serving chicken, rice, and carrots. You place the food on the plate and put it in front of your child. At this point, your toddler might be ready for you to start your usual litany of "eat, eat, eat." Just imagine how surprised she will be when you don't comment on how much or what she eats. Instead, start a normal conversation on anything but food. If after twenty minutes or so your toddler isn't eating, I'd take the plate away and say, "I see you aren't hungry." Don't try offering another menu plan, such as "How about a peanut butter sandwich and tomato soup?"

Also, don't give your toddler creative culinary choices, for example, "Do you want oatmeal or pancakes for breakfast?" While you certainly want your child to be a decision maker, offering alternatives in daily routines such as eating, dressing, and sleeping can really drive you crazy. A toddler is trying so hard to separate from his parents that he very well may fight over every choice.

In the beginning of the year at the Toddler Center the parents always laugh when they hear that our only snack is plain rice cakes. "Oh, my child will never touch that stuff," is the typical comment. Yet over the years very few toddlers have refused these cakes. The reason: I believe strongly that children will eat almost anything if you don't get into a power struggle with them.

However, if your toddler is making meals into a nightmare, refusing to eat or wanting only sweets, you first need to figure out how this power struggle started. Do you think that "good parents" always have "good eaters"? Are you really worried that your child won't grow to be strong? Did your own parents make you clean a plate heaped high with food?

Like many issues in parenting, feeding is a mutual experience. Just as you have the power to select the food, you have to give your child the power to refuse food. A toddler who feels free to be independent will almost always turn out to be a good eater.

Family Meals: Come and Get It

What could be a better time to interact as a family than when you are sitting around the table at mealtimes? Sharing food together is a great introduction to the joys of socializing for a toddler, so concentrate on enjoying each other. While your parents, in-laws, and even some friends may not approve, mealtime is a time to forget about table manners and peace and quiet.

We all know that eating with a toddler isn't often relaxing; a sense of humor is essential. If you expect your child to participate in long group discussions, you and he will go crazy. Let him get up and play when he's finished eating. I know one family with a two-year-old who eat most of their meals outdoors on a picnic table when the weather's good. Says the father: "Our daughter loves to eat, partly, I think, because she loves these casual meals. We also can keep an eye on her as she runs all over the grass."

If you grew up in a family where there was always fighting at meals, where children were expected to be seen and not heard, or where you were quizzed on how much you knew about current events, you may find it difficult to start a new tradition, but you'll find the rewards worth it. Save your arguments until after dessert. Stress may cause your child to nervously overeat or to refuse food.

When both parents work, family meals are obviously not going to be an everyday affair. But whenever possible, for example, on weekends and perhaps for weekday breakfasts, try to make time to eat together as a family. Says one mother: "My husband and I come home from work after my children have eaten. But a few times during the week they have a second dinner with us."

This emphasis on family togetherness may sound as though you and your partner have to give up your romantic candlelit dinners. On the contrary, these cozy encounters are necessary to be happy parents. Let's admit it, conversations are a bit different when your toddler is there. So what about sitting down with a cup of coffee while your toddler eats dinner and saving your appetite for after his bedtime? Your toddler cares about your company, not whether you are eating. Remember, if you aren't home during the day, be sure to ask your caregiver to join your toddler at meals.

Many parents tell me their most persistent memory of meals is that of their mother always standing by the stove preparing the food but never sitting down with them. In television commercials today the mothers (and sometimes the fathers) still rarely seem to pull out a seat for themselves. This frenetic running around by the parents passes the message to their toddler that meals are just for eating, not for speaking.

Parents who take their cooking very seriously and spend vast amounts of time on complicated preparations are bound to feel hurt or angry when their toddler doesn't appreciate their efforts. Either their child won't eat a decent portion, or she'll play with the food, or worse yet she'll tell you she prefers peanut butter to your masterpiece.

Simplicity goes a long way. Meals are much more relaxing if you have them ready before your toddler sits down. There's certainly nothing wrong in buying take-out food once in a while. Or, involve your toddler in the cooking and setup. It's better for your toddler to have a less impressive dinner if it means that she gets her parents' company. Says one mother: "I used to spend an hour or so rushing around getting the meal together and then serving it to my two-and-a-half-year-old. He kept calling to me while I was in the kitchen, but I felt too involved to talk. Then I figured out that I would get him to help set the table and cook. We have great fun together. So what if the food wouldn't pass muster with an adult gourmet."

Food as a Reward or Bribe: I'll Give You a Lollipop If You Don't Cry

It seems that very few parents can resist bringing food treats—from Twinkies to Tootsie Rolls—for their toddler. Sometimes the food is given as a reward, sometimes as a bribe, or sometimes just to make their two-year-old happy. Sugar, in particular, seems to be the essential ingredient in these love treats.

One mother I know gave her two-year-old lollipops every time he didn't cry when she dropped him off at school; another mother gave her daughter a chocolate kiss every time she went on the potty; one father got his son to the doctor by promising to buy a soda on the way home.

It is very tempting to offer your toddler food when she is on the verge of embarrassing you with a temper tantrum or seems unable to listen to reason. Food—especially ice cream, cake, and candy—usually guarantees instant obedience and smiles. Even doctors used to give children lollipops (now it's usually stickers and toys).

In my experience, however, when you use food as a reward, you give it the power to make a child happy or sad. Food may then become an emotional crutch he turns to for comfort. If you want to buy your child a popsicle, buy it without strings attached, not because your child was "good." While food may make a child feel good momentarily, it never brings true self-esteem.

If you find that your toddler is constantly asking for treats all day, then you have probably gotten into the habit of offering food when she is good, hurt, or sad. Can you think of other ways to make your child happy besides feeding her? When she begs for ice cream for the tenth time in ten minutes, how about giving her attention with a big hug or a story? It is not easy, but gradually she won't come to expect a reward of food for all her actions.

Healthy Foods and Portions

The best way to guarantee that your child eats a well-balanced diet is to serve a variety of healthy foods at meals. You don't have to worry if your child doesn't eat something from each of the basic food groups (fruit, vegetables, dairy, grain, meat, fish, poultry) every day. According to the American Academy of Pediatrics, your child is doing fine if he manages to consume something from each group every two to three days. However, keep offering foods that he swears he will never eat. Just because he doesn't like vegetables today doesn't mean that he won't eat them tomorrow. By the age of two, your toddler should be eating almost everything the rest of the family eats.

Remember also that your toddler's tastes aren't set in stone. Although she might happily down a bowl of chicken soup every night, it is important to introduce different types of food. This is the age when children are discovering their food preferences. A little creativity can also work wonders. One father recalls how his daughter detested vegetables until he started putting salad dressing on them.

Try not to load down your toddler's plate at snack and meal times. Give her the chance to let you know when she wants seconds, whether it's by pointing or shouting a loud "more." Serving food in communal family bowls instead of placing individual portions on plates may be more enticing to your toddler precisely because it allows him some control over the amounts. Remember, toddlers can get all their necessary daily vitamins and minerals from very small portions (less than a fistful).

▼ ▼ ▼ ▼ ▼ ▼ ▼ ▼ ▼ ▼ ▼ ▼ ▼ ▼ ▼ ▼ ▼ ▼

Avoid These Tidbits

1. "Just one more bite."

2. "If you don't eat that spinach you can't have dessert."

3. "What would you like to eat?"

4. "If you can't eat properly you won't eat."

5. "If you're good I'll buy you a special candy snack."

6. "If you're bad there is no dessert today."

Table Manners

First of all, don't expect them. By grown-up standards all toddlers have horrible table manners. They lick their fingers, spill constantly, chew with their mouths open, and often mix disgusting-looking concoctions together.

However difficult it may sometimes be to watch your child eat, I don't think toddlerhood is the time to teach etiquette. What's important is for your child to learn to enjoy eating. I can guarantee that she's not going to have good associations with meals if you are constantly correcting her manners.

Make meals easy for your toddler. Serve some finger food (chicken legs, carrot sticks, hard-boiled eggs, bananas, etc.) at every meal. While some toddlers are able to eat with a fork and spoon, many aren't physically capable of using utensils. Your child is going to feel much better about himself and food if he feeds himself instead of having a grown-up shovel every bite into his open mouth. But do give him a toddler-size fork and spoon at every meal just in case he wants to practice, as he probably will. Two-year-olds learn through manipulating their environment.

Also be sure to give your toddler a cup of milk, juice, or water at each meal. Your child's sense of independence is worth a dribble or spill on the floor now and then. Start out with cups with a spout and then work your way up to regular glasses. If you have given her a lot of practice, by two or so she probably will be able to use a glass without too much mess.

"Stevie just *loves* ice cream and cake!"

At the Toddler Center there are always some children who immediately dump their apple juice on the floor during snack time. Instead of making a big deal of their spills we quietly hand them a sponge to help clean up while refilling their glasses (this time with just a smidgen of juice). When the grown-ups don't overreact, most of the children give up their habit by the third day. Interestingly, many of them come from households where there are very rigid rules about table manners. Therefore, these self-respecting toddlers have to make sure they prove their independence at school by spilling.

You can't expect your toddler to patiently sit as adults linger over their food at meals. Let him leave the table when he is no longer eating (even if he's done in three minutes flat) or you'll end up with a food player. Most children play with their food when they aren't hungry or they are bored. So, if you see your toddler fiddling with her meal try saying: "I see you aren't hungry. Let me help you out of the high chair."

Some parents may worry and wonder how their messy little

eater is ever going to make it into respectable society. The truth is, your child will develop good table manners if you have good ones. If you keep eating along with your sloppy, noisy toddler, she'll eventually learn by imitating you.

What to Allow

It may be hard to accept, but many people in your child's life are going to have almost as much control as you over her eating. Friends, teachers, baby-sitters, grandparents, and other parents are all going to offer food to your child. If you are following my advice and don't get overly involved in what your child eats, then you'll feel more relaxed in these situations.

For example, if your child has a playdate at a friend's house, don't worry about what she eats as a snack. You might not keep Oreos in your house, but I would let your daughter eat them at her friend's house.

We all know stories of people who weren't allowed to eat sweets as children, but who eat them constantly as adults. For instance, one mother was adamant about her toddler not eating any sugar. Even at birthday parties her son wasn't allowed a bite of cake or candy. Now forty years old, the man confesses when he's alone he gobbles three or four desserts in one sitting.

If you make a big deal out of a food it often seems to become a child's favorite. When you give your toddler a cupcake, don't make it seem as if you are handing him the royal jewels.

Snacks

You don't want your toddler climbing slides and running ragged on an empty stomach. Many children who eat three meals a day are genuinely hungry and need a snack in midmorning and in mid-afternoon.

However, it's important that you don't make the day into one long meal. I know many parents who offer snacks constantly because they worry that their child has not eaten enough at mealtimes. Says one mother: "If I didn't give my daughter snacks she would starve. She eats like a bird at meals, so I really need to make sure she makes up with snacks."

If your toddler feels she can nibble whenever she wants she'll never eat at meals. You will become a slave not only to the kitchen, but also to her ever-changing taste buds. Says the same mother: "Some days my daughter does drive me crazy. First it's peanut butter, then five minutes later it's bananas, then as soon as I hand her these snacks it's 'No, I don't like any of these.' "

Now is the time to get your toddler into healthy, lifelong eating habits. If you feed him only cookies and chips for snacks it's going to be hard to convert him to nutritious foods later on. If you always deny her junk food she probably will crave it, especially when she sees her friends' goodies. You might try giving him a few cookies along with snacks of fruit, cheese, and our favorite Toddler Center treat, rice cakes.

▼ ▼ ▼ ▼ ▼ ▼ ▼ ▼ ▼ ▼ ▼ ▼ ▼ ▼ ▼ ▼ ▼ ▼
Eating and Emotions

Love

Meg was a firstborn daughter. Her mother had a hard time showing her feelings to her daughter. She worked part-time, but even on her days off seemed to prefer being out of the house to being with Meg. Her father was warm, but seemed to lose interest after playing for a short time.

From day one Meg's parents and baby-sitter used food to make her feel content. They overfed her so she would sleep; they gave her food when she whined. By the time she was two years old, Meg's main interest in life was eating, nurturing herself.

Anger

Three-year-old Greg was very angry because he was going to a summer playgroup every morning. He had just spent a wonderful two-week vacation with his parents and eight-month-old brother. But now they were back, everyone going separate ways.

When Greg's mother picked him up from the playgroup, he immediately had a temper tantrum, calling out for all sorts of food. "I want ice cream. I want candy. Get me a coke. I'm so thirsty."

The mother made this interpretation: "You want something to make you feel better. Anything. You feel so angry with me that you are at the playgroup. It is so hard to come back from a close vacation with Mommy and Daddy. I know just how you feel. It's hard for me, too."

After hearing his mother's explanation repeatedly for four days when he demanded food, Greg's issue with food resolved itself.

Separation Anxiety

Two-and-a-half-year-old Jack suddenly started to overeat at his playgroup. He asked for crackers all morning long and was never satisfied. His eating binge was connected to the fact that his mother and father were on a business trip for three days. He really missed them. Once Jack's parents returned home and spent more time with him he felt better. His endless appetite decreased.

Happiness

Food was the center of every happy event in Diane's house. People cooked for weeks before every holiday. Family time together was spent going out to restaurants. When the children got good report cards or behaved well at relatives' houses, they were always rewarded with sweets. The definite message to the toddler and her siblings was that food is the key to happiness.

▲ ▲ ▲ ▲ ▲ ▲ ▲ ▲ ▲ ▲ ▲ ▲ ▲ ▲ ▲ ▲ ▲ ▲ ▲

Overeating: Weight Watchers, Here We Come

There are certainly some children who seem born loving to eat everything in sight. In past generations people would often say that a child was overweight because of body structure and leave it at that. However, today we want healthy kids whose arteries aren't filled with fatty goo. Many medical experts are now also thinking that fat cells formed in childhood don't go away with age.

While it can be really hard to tease out whether your child is eating out of love for food or an emotional need, it's important to think through what eating represents in your house. Are you giving food when you can give a hug? Are you giving food when you return home from work because you missed your toddler so much? (You're right, it's a separation problem on your part.) Says one father: "Looking back, from the minute Ben was born we used food because it was easier. It started with me stuffing him with formula in the hope that he would sleep longer at night. Then the minute he cried during the day we would bring out the bottle. No wonder my two-year-old is now overweight and when he's slightly upset wants to eat."

Are you on a diet or very conscious of weight? If you seem to be perpetually on a diet, you may either overfeed your toddler to make up for your deprivation or constantly restrict her food. The result: Your toddler may overeat just to get your goat or to please you.

Once you resolve your own issues about food, you should be able to keep your toddler at a healthy weight by (1) limiting junk food and fatty foods; (2) serving small amounts; and (3) making sure your toddler gets plenty of exercise. Also, you should not assume that your child is overweight just because he looks chubbier than his friends. Talk to your pediatrician. It may just be that you have your own views about how thin your toddler should be.

By the way, I would not refer to any of this regime as a diet, because you don't want to give your child a negative image of herself. Also, you don't want to count every calorie she eats. One mother who was always a bit overweight diligently counted up every calorie her two-and-a-half-year-old daughter ate. If the toddler ate what her mother considered a hefty caloric lunch, then dinner was yogurt or cottage cheese. The daughter, needless to say, overate when her mother wasn't around.

Now a Word About Junk Food

No matter how diligently you try to serve nutritious meals or lecture on the evils of sugar, if your cupboards are filled with potato chips and cookies there is probably no way your child is going to become a healthy eater, nor, for that matter, will the rest of the family. It's amazing how children and adults can sniff out a supply of goodies. Consider one mother's story: "My son barely ate at meals because he was stuffing himself all day with chocolate chip cookies. When he was about four years old I took him to an endocrinologist because he just didn't seem to be growing right. The doctor took one look at him and said, 'I think this is the first middle-class kid I've ever seen with malnutrition.' " The moral: Yes, try not to interfere with how much your child eats, but also make sure that what he eats is healthy.

A toddler really can learn to enjoy healthy food if that's what he's served. In the name of health, try limiting the amount of sugar, fat, and salt in the house. Then you won't spend half the day setting restrictions on how much junk food your child can eat. Says one father: "It felt like we were negotiating all day saying, 'Okay, you can have one sweet now but not another one until dinner.' Now that we've changed what we buy, who cares if our daughter eats four carrots and two yogurts!"

Unfortunately, restricting junk food seems to be an obsession among many families. Many parents seem almost to panic when their child even stands near a cookie package. All this extremism only seems to make a toddler crave and obsess about the forbidden fruit. The big thing is not to become too upset about what your toddler eats. A cookie or two on a daily basis is not going to destroy your child. I'd go ahead and offer her two cookies on a plate.

Bottles and Pacifiers

Many experts say that the ideal situation is to skip bottles altogether by weaning a child from the breast to the cup by the age of one year. However, of the hundreds of toddlers that have attended Barnard's Toddler Center, very few have followed this route. So, let's deal with reality. Many toddlers are on bottles until they are three years old. (Firstborn children are sometimes on bottles until they are four years of age.)

Almost all toddlers cling to some comfort object—a bottle, thumb, pacifier, or blanket—when they are sad, tired, or scared. Don't be alarmed if your child needs to soothe herself by sucking on a bottle or lugging around a blanket throughout toddlerhood. Sooner or later she will give up her security. (The most extreme example I know is one woman who threw away her baby blanket the night before her wedding.)

However, just like being toilet trained, getting off the bottle and pacifier can bring your toddler a tremendous sense of self-esteem. Most toddlers feel proud of every accomplishment that makes them feel more independent. In our culture, drinking bottles and using pacifiers is often viewed as an infantile habit. However, as with many other issues in parenting, you need to decide what your attitudes are toward bottles and pacifiers. Some parents think bottles and pacifiers are no big deal, others can't wait to get their toddler off them.

Before you start the process of getting your toddler off bottles or pacifiers, think about when you give him one. Is it for your convenience so you can talk on the phone? Or is it once again a case of making him happy? Is a bottle or pacifier replacing love and patience? Is your child using the bottle to numb all her scared feelings? One child in the Toddler Center spent every morning crying. It turned out that on the days he wasn't at the Center he was given a bottle when his mother left for work and was basically kept on bottles for the rest of the day. The bottle had become a substitute for his mother. When we all realized what was going on, the parents cut down on their son's bottle drinking. The result was that soon he began participating and enjoying his time at school.

If you decide that you are ready to get your toddler off the bottle or the pacifier, you need to talk about it with your child. You might try saying something simple, such as: "When children get to be two and a half they stop drinking from their bottle. Sometimes it can be a little hard to stop. We will try to help you stop. Then soon you will drink from a grown-up cup just like Mommy and Daddy."

For most bottle and pacifier addicts, it works better to begin by gradually cutting down rather than going cold turkey. According to current views of the American Academy of Pediatrics, toddlers need only about two to three cups of milk or the equivalent calcium a day. Offer the cup when your toddler demands more than three bottles a day. You might try setting a rule that no pacifiers or bottles can be taken outside the house.

The ideal situation, of course, would be for your child to wean herself. I know one boy who put all his bottles in the garbage when he was almost three years old. (He happened to have a seven-year-old sister who mercilessly teased him.) Unfortunately, self-weaning doesn't occur very often. Eventually, after you have cut down on the bottles or pacifiers, you will probably reach a point where your toddler will have to go cold turkey.

Getting your child off the bottle or pacifier successfully requires patience and understanding. You also have to believe, without ambivalence, that you are doing the right thing or it won't work. If you have any hesitation about whether this is the right time to kick the habit, your toddler probably won't give it up. You will be torn apart every time (and there will be many times) she cries out for a bottle or pacifier. Relates one father: "We tried a few times when our daughter was two and a half to get her off the bottle. She screamed and made such a fuss that we couldn't go through with it. She also always seemed to get some minor sickness just when she was off the bottle. Finally when she was three we decided this was it. We told her that we weren't taking any bottles away on vacation with us. We were resigned that this would be a vacation in hell. To our surprise she asked for her bottle only once. She knew we meant business and she was ready to get off."

Many parents say that their child doesn't want to drink milk when it is no longer in a bottle. It's important to find other calcium equivalents, such as yogurt, cheese, sardines, or spinach, that your child finds appealing. Also, keep serving milk at every meal. Once the initial shock of finding that milk doesn't come only in bottles is over, your toddler will probably go back to it.

Undereating

Parents can feel terribly worried and guilty if their toddler is in the lowest percentile of weight gain. It can be hard to believe that your child isn't starving if she looks all skin and bones to you.

First, of course, you should always check all your medical concerns with your pediatrician. If your doctor tells you that your child is healthy I would do what might seem to go against the grain of good parenting. Once again, offer good, nutritious food at meals and really try to ignore how much she eats.

One mother in my parent group had a three-year-old daughter who was extremely skinny. In fact, she was so thin that the pediatrician periodically had the girl checked out in the hospital. From day one it became apparent that the mother, who was also very thin, was extremely involved in every bite her daughter took. The girl continued to have eating problems until her mother eased up as a result of divine intervention: a new baby. Not surprisingly, the girl started to eat on her own. The mother also started to interact with her in a more positive way instead of concentrating on her only when she ate. Not eating had been her best way of gaining attention. The girl now became more outspoken and happy.

▼ ▼ ▼ ▼ ▼ ▼ ▼ ▼ ▼ ▼ ▼ ▼ ▼ ▼ ▼ ▼ ▼ ▼ ▼ ▼

Common Concerns

Q: My daughter refuses to eat in her high chair. In fact, she won't eat unless she sits in my lap.

To many toddlers, a mother's lap is the most comforting seat in the world. But if your daughter refuses to eat in her high chair, this could be a separation issue. Have you been spending less time with her recently? If so, maybe some extra hugs and play will make her less clingy. Granting half her wish at mealtimes may help: "You can sit in my lap for a few minutes but then I want you to eat in your high chair."

This situation may have arisen because your daughter is allowed to snack throughout the house. Try restricting eating to one room and one chair. (Some toddlers prefer a booster seat to a high chair.) But once again, don't make a fuss over what she eats. If after fifteen minutes or so she isn't eating, take her out of the chair and say simply, "I see you aren't hungry."

Q: My son spends his entire meal asking for dessert. Should I give him dessert if he doesn't eat his other food?

This sounds like a power struggle to me. If dessert wasn't such a big deal I don't think your son would be so adamant about it. Is dessert held out as a special reward if he cleans his plate? Is dessert always a forbidden treat, like candy or cake?

What about giving your son some of his dessert at the beginning of the meal? Although this is far-fetched, my Uncle Babe was allowed to eat his apple pie before his main course. This kept him satisfied and helped cool the power struggle.

Q: My toddler can't seem to sit still during mealtimes.

This is a typical complaint from parents unless they have a child who really loves to eat. First of all, your expectations may be off.

Your toddler probably is not as interested in food as you are. She may finish eating in about five minutes.

I have also noticed that many children who want to get up and down from the table have been forced to sit there for an unreasonable amount of time. Let your toddler leave the table when she's finished eating.

Q: My child seems to eat his meals walking around.

I think every family should have one designated place of eating, preferably at a table with everyone else in the family. As you've read frequently in this book, I believe that meals are a time to talk and laugh together. If your toddler becomes a wandering bedouin during meals he'll miss out on all the great talk and you'll spend half your time cleaning up his crumbs.

Q: Do you think it is bad for my daughter to watch TV while she eats?

No child should regularly eat her meals in front of the television. Meals are a time to feel close to the family, not to Big Bird and his gang. Watching television during meals hinders socialization.

Your child also could become so absorbed by TV that she won't even realize what she's eating. Eating will become a mindless exercise rather than a sensory experience.

Q: My son makes such a mess when he eats. What should I do?

Hard as it can be, I would ignore the mess as long as your son is eating. Putting down a plastic splat mat under his chair should help save your carpets.

However, I don't think toddlers should be creative chemists with food. If your son is playing with his food and not eating, I would simply take the plate away and say: "Food is for eating. I see you are not hungry."

Q: My son drinks several bottles during the day. Could they be destroying his appetite?

If your child is getting all his calories from milk, he is going to be too full to eat at meals. Most doctors say toddlers need no more than about two to three cups of milk a day or the calcium equivalent. If your son is drinking more than that, he is probably not going to be hungry.

You also might think about gradually taking away the bottles. A first step would be offering a cup rather than a bottle when he is thirsty.

Q: My two-year-old asks for peanut butter sandwiches at every meal.

Two-year-olds love the tried and true. If you've been giving your toddler choices of food at mealtimes, this very well may be where you and she will end up. However, if you are in this situation, give in to the peanut butter obsession. (Of course, be sure to put some other food of your choice on her plate.) Your toddler won't want peanut butter forever, and besides, it is relatively healthy.

Q: My daughter can't seem to stop eating. She always wants more.

Some kids grab toys, your daughter goes for the food. Say something like: "I see you need it all. I wish I could give you all the food at once." Then try giving her a cracker for each hand.

Q: My caregiver wants to take my toddler to McDonald's for lunch every Friday with some friends. What should I do? I try not to give her junk food.

If you are really against the food at McDonald's, maybe your caregiver would consider a pizza parlor. You also can limit how often she goes to McDonald's. Do you think once a week is excessive?

It's important for your toddler to become socialized. What could be a better way than sharing a meal with friends? Although it is also important to give your toddler a nutritious diet, it's okay to yield a bit in the name of socialization.

Q: It really bothers me that parents give candy at parties. I don't allow my son to eat sweets.

Hang loose. Remember, you are living in a world where grown-ups and children eat sweets. If you don't allow your child to eat some of the candy he will feel deprived. He very well may crave sweets. Food could become a power issue.

Q: We don't have a regular baby-sitter and would like to take our daughter out to eat with us. What should we expect?

First of all, don't make reservations at the fanciest restaurant in town. Pick a family restaurant or a restaurant that is noisy enough to prevent diners from being bothered by a boisterous toddler. Expect your child to act just as she acts at home, probably spilling food and wanting to get down from the table after ten minutes or so. So, will you enjoy dining out? That depends on your tolerance level, your daughter's ability to eat in a new environment and how much you really want to go out.

Summary

Starting at birth, feeding a child is one of the major sources of joy and angst for parents. It is a way for a parent to nurture, comfort, and give love. Eating is also an activity that is totally in the toddler's control.

Most children who develop eating difficulties seem to do so because parents become too involved. Food becomes a rock-hard power struggle. The best way of avoiding or getting out of this struggle is to let your toddler decide how much she wants to eat. A grown-up's only power should be to select and cook the food.

Difficulties also can arise when parents use food to reward or comfort, instead of dealing directly with their child's emotions, laughing with her when she is happy, consoling him with hugs when he's sad. Like so many other issues in early childhood, how parents were brought up is going to affect their attitudes. For instance, did you have to be a member of the clean-plate club?

Family meals are a wonderful way to naturally introduce the joys of socializing. I believe that the main purpose of a meal should be to concentrate on enjoying each other, rather than on how much and what your toddler eats.

▼ ▼ ▼ ▼ ▼ ▼ ▼ ▼ ▼ ▼ ▼ ▼ ▼ ▼ ▼ ▼ ▼ ▼

CHAPTER 6

Sleeping

WHAT BETTER WAY FOR A FAMILY TO HELP THEIR toddler achieve independence than by encouraging him to learn to sleep alone. Sleep provides a natural opportunity to foster the separation process, because at least eight hours every day of the year a toddler does it. While many books offer helpful tips, I believe that the key to understanding your child's bedtime habits is viewing them as issues of separation.

Sleep is a problem for toddlers precisely because it coincides with their developmental task of becoming separate from you. And of course, nothing during this age comes easily. Sleeping alone in a room without a mother or father can bring out all a toddler's anxieties about being on his own.

It's understandable that sleep-deprived parents want their child's bedtime issues resolved immediately. When parents reach the point where they can't stand another night of exhaustion, it can be hard to be patient. But remember that a toddler will not become a good sleeper overnight. This chapter includes suggestions that should help in the ups and downs of sleep, but they are not a total cure for problems. Separation is a slow process affected by how

"Ok, heads I get the crib, tails you do."

parents react to their toddler's growing independence. For instance, do you feel lonely or worried when your child isn't right next to you? Like toilet training and giving up bottles or pacifiers, a child learns how to be a good sleeper when she feels that her parents have faith in her ability to become one.

Additionally, what happens during a toddler's day is going to affect his night. If he had a fight with his friend or if he has a new baby-sitter, he very well might spend half the night calling out for his parents. Or if he didn't get enough hugs and cuddles because his parents were out most of the day, he might wake to get them. Some children will never become long sleepers no matter what their mother and father do. While many toddlers sleep between twelve and fourteen hours daily, others do quite well on eight to ten hours.

Every family must decide on what sleeping arrangements are best suited to their own beliefs and cultural standards. Do you think a baby should stay in her parents' room until she is one? Or do you think a three-month-old should be sleeping in her crib in her own room? Were you brought up sharing a room with siblings? Did your parents not mind you spending part of the night in bed with them?

Or were you one of those children who always enjoyed cuddling up under your blanket with your teddy bear in your own bed? It may be hard to believe when your toddler cries out for you at 3 A.M., but sleep can be another source of pleasure, solace, and joy for your toddler just as playing, eating, running, and talking can be.

Parents' Sleep History

If you have always fallen asleep easily and can't think of anything more enjoyable than a night of blissful sleep, chances are some of this good fortune should rub off on your toddler.

If, however, you find that going to bed seems to stir up your own anxieties, your toddler might pick up some of your difficulties with sleep. This father's experience speaks for many: "I have always been an insomniac. All my worries seem to surface at night. I am usually tense when I put my two-and-a-half-year-old to sleep because I'm already thinking that he is going to wake up. I have such trouble sleeping that all I need is for my child to keep me up."

Not surprisingly, this father's worries have become a self-fulfilling prophecy. He is anxious lest his son won't sleep; the son goes to bed feeling his father's distress; and the night becomes one long up-and-down confrontation.

If you also had parents who made bedtime an unpleasant experience through unreasonably strict routines you may unintentionally make your toddler feel that bedtime is not enjoyable. Recalls one mother: "I went to bed when it was light outside and I could still hear my friends playing. As a result I fought sleep all the time and now with my toddler it is hard for me to set a strict bedtime."

For parents like this mother and father who feel jittery just hearing the word *sleep*, it makes sense to let a more relaxed partner (if there is one) handle most of the bedtime routine.

Routine: It May Be Boring but It Works

Routines may be tedious for parents (365 nights of the same books, the same nighttime farewell) but they make a toddler feel secure. It comforts a two-year-old to know that first she has dinner, then a warm bath, two stories, a snack, teeth brushed, and bed. She feels that she can trust and knows what to expect of her environment. Routine helps a child feel calm enough to sleep.

Many parents of good sleepers often seem to have their toddler on a routine without knowing it. "Routine! I don't do anything special. I give her an old baby blanket, hold her for a minute or two, sing one verse of 'Twinkle Twinkle Little Star.' That's it," says one mother.

Whatever the ritual, try to keep it simple and low-key. You don't want a complicated process that takes up half the evening and causes parents to count every minute until bedtime. For example, choose the number of books before you do any reading. Don't overexcite your toddler with rough-and-tumble play fifteen minutes before his bedtime. It's going to be hard for him to suddenly shift into a drowsy mood. And although television may temporarily quiet down your toddler, it can also stimulate him and sometimes bring on nightmares.

It's important for you and your partner to agree on all the details of the routine, since the whole point of having one is that they are calming. Says one father: "My son was not sleeping well and we couldn't figure out why. Suddenly one night I realized my wife and I were always squabbling over the bedtime routine. When it's her turn to put our son to sleep, she reads many more books, sings many more songs, gives many more kisses—it feels interminable and almost like a competition to me." The couple then sat down together and worked out a routine with which they both felt comfortable.

Avoiding Trouble Spots

I believe it is the parents' job to create the right atmosphere when their toddler goes to sleep. Bedtime is not a good time to yell at your child or partner, have long phone conversations, or fail to give your toddler the attention he needs. Very few children sleep well if they feel tense, unhappy, or neglected.

From early on, help your child feel that her bed is somewhere she can go to enjoy her own thoughts. Parents can help make a bed a happy place by putting one or two favorite stuffed animals and a beloved blanket in it. Don't use the crib or bed as a punishment. Your toddler will obviously not have fond associations with her bed if you send her to it when she is "bad."

But by far the most important way a parent can help a toddler is by letting him learn how to fall asleep on his own. For example, if you have always rocked your child to sleep, try holding him, patting him slowly, and then putting him down when his eyes are still open. If you have always let your daughter fall asleep with the bottle, try giving her a bottle in a dim room and then putting her to bed without the bottle before she has actually fallen asleep. Says one father: "Our daughter was so used to sleeping with the bottle that if she woke up at all in the night she would instantly shout out, 'Bottle.' At one point she was having four bottles a night! She had no idea how to fall asleep without one."

Not surprisingly, first-time parents usually have the most problems with sleep. It can be so hard to leave a small, cuddly child alone in the dark. "There was no more wonderful sensation than feeling that tiny baby when I held her in my arms and rocked her to sleep," says one mother. But by the second year, most parents no longer feel so sentimental about nighttime closeness. Later, from this same mother: "My daughter no longer feels so wonderful in my arms because I'm exhausted! Not only do I have to rock this thirty-pound child for one hour at night, but if she wakes up I have to do it once again." This parent had obviously reached her limits. Within one week she had started a campaign to get her daughter to fall sleep in her crib.

Saying Good Night

Saying good night can be very hard when your child is clingy, weepy, or angry. But if you don't set limits, bedtime will become a long-drawn-out drama every night.

Once you finish your nighttime ritual and get your child into her bed, try calmly and firmly saying something like: "Night night. It's time for you to sleep." Give a kiss and then leave the room, keeping the door open. If you use a night-light, make sure it doesn't cast any scary shadows.

Now, wouldn't it be nice if getting a toddler to sleep were really this simple? But unless your toddler is feeling extraordinarily exhausted or generous, expect a callback until he sees that his parents mean business. How many of us have heard that nightly "Mommy, Mommy. Daddy, Daddy!"

I'd first try answering his call from outside his room: "It really is time to sleep. Mommy and Daddy are close by in the next room. Good night."

But once again your toddler probably won't let you off so easily. He now may really start crying. Parents have their own tolerance for how long they can stand hearing their toddler cry. (Ferber's book, *Solve Your Child's Sleep Problems,* offers some helpful advice.) I'd try to wait ten minutes or so after the first return. Certainly a little crying will never make a child feel horrible about sleeping. Go back in and, if possible without taking him out of the crib or turning on the light, briefly reassure him that he can fall asleep on his own. "Now it is time to go to sleep. I know you can do it." The main thing is not to give your toddler any hope of fun. You may have to visit his room half a dozen times before he finally gets the message that it really is time to sleep.

Even if you don't make it through the night without taking your toddler out of his bed, at least you are on your way to helping support his separation. If your toddler gets out of bed on his own, immediately take him back to his room and stay with him until he calms down.

Waking Up in the Night

Whenever a toddler wakes up and cries in the night, it's a good idea for her parents to acknowledge her distress by calling out from their bedroom. True, a crying child will eventually go to sleep when parents don't respond. But a simple "I'm here for you. Now go to sleep," can be very comforting without making your toddler feel that she must have you in person. What you are trying to do is give your toddler the experience of falling back asleep alone. I'm told this long-distance call eventually does work.

If you really feel you need to go in, try calming her without taking her out of her bed. In a soft, firm voice say: "Mommy and Daddy are sleeping. The birds are sleeping. Grandma is sleeping. Your teddy bear is sleeping. I love you very much. But I am going to sleep now." Then reassure her, and probably yourself, with a light pep talk: "I have great faith in your ability to go to sleep."

According to doctors, children have some periods of wakefulness during the night. However, if your toddler is continually waking up, it is important to think about any recent changes that may be disturbing his sleep. For instance, has he started a new playgroup? Is he coming down with a cold? Was his sleep routine thrown off because of dinner guests? Have you been away from home for his bedtime the last two nights?

There comes a point when some parents can't stand these nightly wake-up scenes anymore. Many parents tell me their only remedy is to go cold turkey when they've reached the end of their rope. When their toddler wakes them up for the fifth time in one hour they don't go to his room, no matter how miserable he sounds.

I suspect the reason this method works is that this is the only way some toddlers know their parents mean business. (And this is the only way some parents know they mean business.)

▼ ▼ ▼ ▼ ▼ ▼ ▼ ▼ ▼ ▼ ▼ ▼ ▼ ▼ ▼ ▼ ▼ ▼ ▼

Keys to Sleeping

1. Don't forget to look at what has happened during your toddler's day when he has a hard night. For instance, talk to him about how he felt when Suzy bit him at the sandbox or he fell off the swing. Reassure him that you are there for him. By talking about your toddler's feelings, you will comfort and reassure him.

2. Don't give yourself a deadline in getting your toddler to be a good sleeper. She probably won't meet it, and you'll only be more tense. Just keep sticking to her routine.

3. Don't lose your cool when your child awakens you at night. You are trying to teach your toddler that he can survive happily on his own. He'll only become agitated if you are furious with his nighttime interruptions.

4. Don't expect your toddler to sleep soundly if there has been a recent disruption in her life, such as a new baby, a new caregiver, or the end of a vacation.

5. Putting your toddler to sleep outside his bed will never teach him how to fall asleep on his own.

6. Think about your own needs before you bring your toddler into your bed. You probably won't sleep well with a two-year-old sprawled across you.

7. Bottles and pacifiers may seem a convenient tool for getting a toddler back to sleep, but your child will end up needing them every time she falls asleep or wakes up.

8. Make sure that you and your partner take turns answering your toddler's late night and early morning wake-up calls.

9. Remember, every family has its own tolerances and beliefs about sleep habits. There isn't one wrong or right way.

Nightmares

A toddler can go though long periods of being awakened by nightmares. He may be reacting to a particularly stressful event that day, or he may simply be experiencing normal two-year-old fears. Toilet training, giving up the bottle, or any push toward independence can set a child off.

If parents can pinpoint the part of their toddler's life that is a strain they can help him through it. For example, if you are over-socializing your toddler by sending him to a playgroup in the morning and a gym class in the afternoon, you might cut down on his activities.

It is also a good idea to monitor books and television. Even the most seemingly harmless cartoons or stories can frighten a sensitive toddler. Says one mother: "I let my two-and-a-half-year-old watch the *Nutcracker Suite* on television. I remembered it as a wonderful fairy tale with beautiful ballerinas. But what did my daughter focus on? The rats! In fact, for weeks she woke up at night with dreams of rats." Read bedtime books with soothing stories and pictures, for example, *Goodnight Moon.*

When your toddler calls out from a dream, you may find her half asleep or sitting up sobbing. Usually you can console a toddler by repeating over and over words of comfort such as "You just had a dream. Dreams aren't real. Mommy and Daddy are here now. Everything is safe."

It also helps to talk with your child the next morning about her dream and dreams in general. You could say something like: "It seems you got scared by a dream last night. Dreams are only pretend stories. Sometimes people have scary ones. But they are not real. If you have a bad dream, Mommy and Daddy will help you not to be scared. You are safe in this house when you sleep."

Night Terrors

Night terrors look like intense versions of nightmares. You may find your toddler sitting up in bed, eyes open but not recognizing you, screaming inconsolably with fear.

First, try talking in a soothing voice. Give her the idea that everything is safe now, that she had a bad dream. You may feel that you have to wake her if she seems inconsolable. One mother told me that the only way she could get her daughter out of the terror was to carry her into the living room and turn on a Mr. Rogers tape.

If the night terrors go on for a long time, consult your pediatrician. While doctors don't know exactly why some children have night terrors, yours may be able to give you specific advice on helping your toddler.

Naps

Nap time should not be negotiable. Every toddler should have some quiet time every day at the same time. Even if he claims he isn't sleepy, he needs to be able to entertain himself quietly for a time. Put a few toys in his bed and say something like: "The rule in this house is that all children take a nap. You don't have to sleep, but it is quiet time."

By two years of age most children need only one nap a day. But if your toddler doesn't have a nap until four o'clock, remember, he probably won't go to sleep until late.

From Crib to Bed

When your toddler starts to climb out of her crib, it's time to buy a bed. You can't count on a toddler's gymnastic prowess to prevent her from having an accident. A fall from a crib onto a hard floor can be dangerous.

Even if your toddler doesn't seem to have any climbing inclinations, I recommend a bed by the time he's around three years old. Beds (much as you may dread them) will be one more way of promoting independence.

Once you bring the bed into his room it's a good idea to get rid of the crib. It can feel confusing for a toddler to see his crib when he is trying to sleep in a grown-up bed. Keeping the crib in the room also increases the chance of a toddler playing musical beds all night.

Be sure to put side rails on the bed. Even toddlers who are sound sleepers often take one too many rolls during the night. Also, now that your child can get out of bed by herself, she may start roaming around at all hours. Examine her room closely to be sure that it is childproof.

The independent freedom of a bed can be frustrating to some parents. Just when you think you have the rest of the evening to read a book or talk with your partner, your toddler suddenly gets out of his bed and reappears by your side. Right away, try calmly and firmly saying: "Do you remember you just said goodnight? It's your job to go to bed now. Mommy and Daddy need some time together. We're going to walk you back to your bed now."

In this situation it is a good idea for both parents to walk their toddler into his room. If your toddler sees that you both mean business and that sleep isn't negotiable, he may climb out of bed a few more times, but in the end calmness and persistence will prevail.

Try not to move your child from a crib to a bed right before any big event. For example, if you plan to put your new baby in your toddler's crib, have your two-and-a-half-year-old move into a bed a few months before the sibling arrives. She then won't feel displaced by the newest family member.

Early Wake-up Call

When you look at your bedside clock at dawn, try to remember that it's because your child loves you that he wants to see you when he opens his eyes. True, you might get a few more winks if you put some toys and books in his crib the night before. And if he is out of the crib and in a bed, he might actually restrain himself for a few seconds if you call out: "Mommy and Daddy are still sleeping. How about playing by yourself for a few minutes until it is time to get up?"

But as all parents know, when a toddler wakes up raring to go, you can prolong your sleep just so long. Most parents can sleep past 7 A.M. only if their partner gets up with the children.

The Family Bed

Some societies and families believe in the communal bed. It seems natural that a toddler would want to be soothed by her parents. This is the purpose of a family. When parents deliberately choose the family bed as a comfortable, satisfying way to raise their children, then I believe it will succeed.

However, a toddler can certainly feel attached to her parents without being with them all night if she receives plenty of hugs, kisses, and empathy during the day. Sleeping alone can also help your toddler feel that she can function on her own and not be sad when she is separated from you.

Problems seem to arise when parents fall into having a family bed because it seems a lot easier than teaching a child how to sleep on his own. Says one mother: "I was getting so exhausted running back and forth to my daughter's crib all night that I just put her in our bed. Now I regret it because she sprawls all over me and I can't sleep. I also can't get her out."

When you become convinced that you want your toddler back in his room, your decisiveness will eventually convince him. You might say something like: "It is time for you to start sleeping in your room again. Mommy and Daddy get a little cranky if they are tired. We need a good night's sleep and so do you. We will be here if you need us."

Waking Up

Does this sound familiar? "My daughter always wakes up grumpy. Sometimes I just dread going into her room. On the other hand, her older brother always seems to wake up incredibly cheerful."

Some toddlers seem to need time to adjust to a new day. A big smile and conversation is just not their style. It doesn't help them or you to take their crankiness personally or feel obligated to get them in a good mood.

Of course, it's important to make sure there isn't something that is making your daughter unhappy about the coming day. Says one mother: "I always thought it was my daughter's nature to wake up in a bad mood. Then I started realizing that she was always in a great mood on the weekends. I put two and two together and concluded that our weekday schedule was too hectic for her. We left for work about fifteen minutes after she got up. Now we wake her up so she can spend an hour with us. She is much happier."

One father whose son always seemed to wake up irritable relates: "My child really just wanted to lounge around the house rather than have a scheduled playgroup routine each morning. I changed our dates to only two mornings per week."

▼ ▼ ▼ ▼ ▼ ▼ ▼ ▼ ▼ ▼ ▼ ▼ ▼ ▼ ▼ ▼ ▼ ▼
Common Concerns

Q: When my daughter is sick, should I bring her into my bed?

Try going into her room and comforting her there. You may end up resting on her floor or in a rocking chair until she falls asleep, but bringing her into your bed will only make it harder to keep her out when she feels better.

Q: My two-year-old daughter wants to stay up with my four-year-old son at night.

If your two-year-old seems to need more sleep than your four-year-old, I would put her to sleep earlier. But every child has different sleep needs. One of the Toddler Center parents says that her older daughter likes to go to sleep before her two-year-old. She reads both of them stories at the same time. She takes the five-year-old to bed and then a half hour later puts her two-year-old to bed.

No matter the bedtimes, it would be nice if you could spend a little time alone with each of your children before putting them to sleep.

Q: My two-and-a-half-year-old son sleeps on a blanket on the floor next to my bed. It's starting to get to me.

You probably started putting the blanket on the floor as a way to ease him out of your bed. Now you seem ready to go on to the next step. If you feel that's the case, have a conversation with him that goes something like this: "I think it is time for you to stay in your own bed in your room. Mommy will read you a story and then put you to sleep. Mommy and Daddy are always nearby when you are sleeping."

If you have really made up your mind that you don't want him in your room, even though he may protest, he will get the message that he will be safe away from you and that a definite limit has been set.

Q: My toddler's sleep habits go crazy when we travel.

You have to expect that your child's sleep pattern will be disrupted when you travel. Some toddlers, however, do fine in new situations and fall asleep as soon as the lights are turned out, whereas others find it very hard to adjust to a new bed, new room, new noises.

Try to stick to your child's bedtime routine, but expect many more nighttime trips to her room. Eventually she will get used to the new environment. Be patient.

Q: My toddler can't seem to go to sleep unless I sit in his room.

As long as you have established some kind of routine, whether it is singing two songs or reading two stories, completion of the routine should mean that it is time to sleep. When you have finished the routine and said good night, walk firmly out of the room with your own mantra: "I know he can do it." Remember, it will take some time for your toddler to develop a new habit of getting to sleep alone.

What you are doing by sitting in the room is passing on the message that it is not safe to go to sleep alone. Again, if you are determined that he go to sleep on his own, he will get the message you mean business.

Q: My toddler keeps calling me back at night with any excuse, usually that he's thirsty.

This is like a vaudeville routine. A toddler will do anything to keep Mom and Dad in the room.

If he is thirsty, obviously you should give him a glass of water. But if a second request for more water occurs ten seconds later, I'd try comforting him by saying something like: "It's night-night time. Everyone is sleeping. We'll get up in the morning and see you then."

Q: I thought my child would sleep better now that she doesn't nap. But it is quite the opposite.

There is a point of no return. Overtired toddlers actually have more difficulty sleeping than they normally have. The tension and excitement just builds up and up.

Most toddlers will fall asleep during nap time. After all, they have been busy running, touching, and exploring the world. However, even if your daughter says she's not tired, give her some quiet time alone in her room. There is nothing like a toddler learning how to entertain herself and enjoy her own company. You also need the break from her.

Q: Since I became pregnant, my two-year-old wants to camp out at night in my room.

Unless you plan to establish a family bed where all members sleep together you need to change the situation now, or when the baby comes your toddler will never move out.

First of all, why is your two-year-old in your bed? If you aren't sure, establish some sleep routines and make sure that he ends up in his own bed. You might be feeling guilty about having the new baby. If so, admitting your own ambivalence about replacing your prince or princess, will also make nighttimes easier.

Q: If I don't go to my son the minute he cries, he makes himself throw up. What should I do?

In the Toddler Center parent groups, this situation comes up more than you might suspect. Some children get their gag reflexes to work overtime when they want their parents. Like every other toddler power struggle, the best thing is to ignore it. Go in the room, change the sheets without commenting on his throwing up, and say, "Now that I've made your bed nice and clean, it's time to go to sleep."

Summary

Parents know that their children need sleep in order to grow and be productive. However, just as eating can become a power struggle so, too, can putting your toddler to sleep. Sleep is not only a way to renew your child physically, but it also gives him the experience of being alone and separate from you in the warm, nesting environment of his crib or bed.

Letting your child learn how to fall asleep on her own helps her feel that she can function by herself. Of course, this lesson entails resolve on your part. You really have to believe that your child is capable of getting to sleep and staying asleep on her own. Rocking your toddler to sleep or being oversolicitous in the good-night routine may be a sign that you need to look into your own history. Was bedtime unpleasant for you as a child? Do you have a hard time falling asleep? Do you find it difficult to separate from your child?

If one night your child suddenly seems to give you a hard time going to sleep or wakes up often, think about what has happenend during the day. Was her favorite wagon grabbed away from her in the playground? Is he coming down with a cold? Were you not home for her bedtime ritual? Don't look at a few setbacks as a sign that your toddler will never sleep again. Also, remember that no child becomes a sound sleeper overnight.

▼ ▼ ▼ ▼ ▼ ▼ ▼ ▼ ▼ ▼ ▼ ▼ ▼ ▼ ▼ ▼ ▼ ▼

CHAPTER 7

Free at Last—
No More Diapers

AVE YOU EVER FELT AS IF THE ENTIRE WORLD WERE checking out your toddler's bulky bottom as he climbed up the jungle gym? Have you spent the last six months obsessing over when and how to toilet train? Do you worry that your child will never be trained in time for nursery school?

So many parents look back and laugh at how competitive and pressured they felt about having their child be the first (or at least not the last) on the block in underpants. They are convinced now that their toddler would have been trained earlier and with much less stress if they hadn't seen toilet training as a sign of being a successful parent. Just as every child learns to walk and talk when she is ready, one day your toddler really will shed her diapers and become toilet trained.

That said, I don't think there is a more appropriate age than between the ages of two and three to start the process. This is the time when a child tests constantly to see who holds the power so that he can figure out who he is. Toilet training can bring a new sense of self-esteem, self-control, and independence to a toddler. "Hey, look at me, I'm doing it all by myself!" From diapers to underpants, you may see an enormous change in your child's personality as he gains control of his body. He could suddenly become very confident and even calm.

Helping your toddler during this period can require enormous amounts of tact, time, patience, and creativity. For the first time, parents may become aware of their child's learning style and their teaching style. You may feel jealous when you see your best friend's twenty-three-month-old head for the potty in stark white underpants. But try not to push your child before she is interested. Your toddler will give you clues, although they may be very subtle, when she is ready (see page 100). Most doctors say that children have to be at least two years old before they have enough muscle control to hold urine in their bladders for a few hours. Also, the older your child, the easier it will be to explain the toileting process and the more pride she will take in her successes. To everything in life there is a season.

What Really Matters

It is easy to become confused with all the books and expert advice available. There is probably more written information on poops and pee pee than on any other single subject of childhood. You may find in the course of your research suggestions, such as blowing bubbles on the potty, or books, such as *Going to the Potty* by Fred Rogers, that inspire your toddler.

But the real success of toilet training comes when parents feel that they are doing the right thing by giving the gift of independence to their toddler. Just as parents wean their child from the breast to the bottle to the cup and from soft baby food to finger food, so they wean him from the diaper onto the toilet.

Although plenty of parents complain about messy diapers, most of us are conflicted about our baby growing up. Many parents feel that diapers are the last farewell to babyhood. Their child now has a real big kid's body, without the adorable bulge in back. This physical look that says "no more baby" can affect how parents feel about their child.

The other crucial aspect of toilet training is that it is a natural bodily event. It's important to make toilet training as relaxed and uncomplicated as possible. What parents don't want their child to have a positive image of his body? One hesitant mother speaks for many when she says, "I'm terrified I'll screw up my son's sexuality and self-esteem forever if I take the wrong approach to toilet training."

If you feel rigid and uncomfortable about toilet training, there's nothing wrong in letting someone else take over—a baby-sitter, grandparent, spouse, day-care center. One mother handed the job to her baby-sitter because her experience training her older son was so disastrous. Every effort to get her three-year-old to use the potty had turned into a screaming battle of control. By the end of toilet training the parents had spent hundreds of dollars on presents to use as rewards for their son and had suffered hours of misery. The baby-sitter didn't carry any of these memories as baggage. She was confident that it would be no big deal to train the two-year-eight-month-old girl. She simply announced that it was time to go pee pee and the child was trained happily and with confidence.

▼ ▼ ▼ ▼ ▼ ▼ ▼ ▼ ▼ ▼ ▼ ▼ ▼ ▼ ▼ ▼ ▼ ▼

Signs of Readiness

A toddler is ready for training if:

1. He announces when he is having a bowel movement or urinating.

2. She is a very appreciative and curious audience when her parents or friends urinate.

3. He is first in line to watch children having their diapers changed.

4. She enjoys playing with water and mushy, gushy materials such as play dough and mud. Many children would love to play with their urine and BMs but instead find parent-accepted substitutes.

5. He refuses to wear diapers.

6. She seems to be aware of almost everything her mother or father does, which means she may be ready to copy her parents in using the toilet.

7. He stays dry for several hours or overnight.

8. She may try to overcompensate for not yet being able to control her body by controlling her environment. For example, she may insist on wearing the same ripped red shirt day after day.

▲ ▲ ▲ ▲ ▲ ▲ ▲ ▲ ▲ ▲ ▲ ▲ ▲ ▲ ▲ ▲ ▲ ▲ ▲ ▲

You Call This Fun?

Toilet training is not a particularly relaxing or enjoyable time for parents or children. Expect your toddler to have volatile moods during toilet training. While she may be proud of her new skills, she's also upset about leaving the soft, cuddly world of babyhood.

Previously you took care of all your toddler's physical needs; you fed and changed him. Although your child is now liberated by controlling his own urine and BMs, he also misses being the baby who had everything done for him.

Don't be surprised if your toddler tests his aim in unusual places, such as on your white rug. Creative peeing is a favorite activity during toilet training. Until your child really gets it, expect a lot of accidents. When these episodes occur, remind your child in a low-key way that pee and poop go in the potty.

▼ ▼ ▼ ▼ ▼ ▼ ▼ ▼ ▼ ▼ ▼ ▼ ▼ ▼ ▼ ▼ ▼ ▼ ▼

Preparing Your Toddler for Training

1. Buy a potty and leave it in the bathroom. Suggest that your child sit on it whenever he wants.

2. Let your child watch you use the toilet.

3. Buy some big kid underpants.

4. Read some children's books about toilet training together.

◆ ◆ ◆ ◆ ◆ ◆ ◆ ◆ ◆ ◆ ◆ ◆ ◆ ◆ ◆ ◆ ◆ ◆

Ready, Set, Go!

1. Toilet training is labor-intensive. Many working parents designate their vacation time as official potty training time. Whether you train your toddler in an idyllic ocean hut or in your house, try picking a period of time when you'll be relatively free of stress or work pressure.

2. Don't overload your toddler. If she has just started at a new playschool or had a new sibling, wait.

3. Explain the process of toilet training by reading books aloud or making up your own special version. The explanation should be low-key and basic. For example: "All animals, children, and grown-ups eat and go pee pee and poopie. When children get to be your age they start to go pee and poo like Mommy and Daddy in the toilet."

4. The days of going to the toilet alone are over. Your toddler learns by watching. Toddlers want to please and copy their parents. They are using the potty because they love you.

5. Buy a child's potty so that he can plant his feet on the floor. The toilet may be easier to clean, but your toddler won't feel as secure. A potty also reduces any anxieties he may have about hearing the toilet flush or falling into the bowl. Let your toddler play with the potty and sit on it whenever he wants. Don't be surprised if, one day, you chance upon a BM in the potty. (It's not the dog!)

6. Get ready for bare bottoms! Toddlers often like the warm, mushy feeling of diapers. Therefore, you may have to do something drastic, such as leaving your toddler naked as much as possible. (You might find it practical to temporarily roll up your rugs at this point.) Children become much more aware of their urine and BMs when they are naked. Once you have begun serious training, I'd recommend that your toddler switch to underpants rather than wear diapers, at least in the daytime.

7. Although some toddlers may march off to the potty independently or tell you when they have to go, most don't for the first few months. Rather than rely on grunts, faraway looks in eyes, or squats in a corner, start a schedule. Take your toddler when he gets up in the morning, after breakfast, at lunch time, after nap, after dinner, and before bath (unless you want urine in the tub).

8. Many toddlers put up less of a fuss if you prepare them in advance by saying something like, "As soon as you finish that painting we'll go to the potty." Remember, you are dealing with a two-year-old who has just learned to say a big "No!" when asked questions.

9. Do whatever is fun for your child. Let her blow bubbles on the potty, decorate the potty with stickers, read, bring a doll.

10. After five to ten minutes if nothing has happened, simply say, "Oh, I see you don't have to go now." You don't want your toddler using the potty as a lounge chair.

11. Encourage the successes, but don't overdo it. Try saying something like, "Oh, I see you really do it, just like Mommy and Daddy." Just as it is routine for your toddler to eat and sleep, so it should not be a big deal for him to use the potty.

These are the basic steps. However, you're in this for the long haul. You'll have to help him take off his clothes, wipe, and make sure he washes his hands.

▲ ▲ ▲ ▲ ▲ ▲ ▲ ▲ ▲ ▲ ▲ ▲ ▲ ▲ ▲ ▲ ▲ ▲ ▲ ▲

Substitute Play

It's always shocking (because most parents can't remember their own experiences) how much children love to play with their body eliminations. Civilization has taught us to subliminate this urge so that it comes across as disgusting.

Children love and admire what they create, especially poops and pees. It does not smell bad nor is it disgusting to them. You can make your child ashamed if you say anything that's even slightly derogatory, for example, "Let's get rid of that yucky poopoo."

Since you can't let your toddler play with urine or BMs, try letting him play with acceptable substitutes, such as paints and play dough. All this play seems to fulfill toddlers' needs during toilet training. At the Toddler Center we put little play toilets on the play dough table, which seems to be very satisfying to the customers.

A toddler can go through gallons of play dough. You can make your own with the following recipe:

2 cups flour
1 cup salt
2 tsp. cream of tartar
4 tb. salad oil
2 cups water with food coloring

Mix everything together in a pot over medium heat until the mixture reaches a heavy consistency. Remove the dough from the pot and knead.

Deadlines

My advice: Don't have them. You'll only drive yourself and your toddler crazy. Of course, it's understandable for you to want your toddler in underwear by the time he starts nursery school or before the new baby arrives. However, this pressure for accomplishment usually backfires. You and your toddler will end up angry with each other and in a major power struggle. A consistent but relaxed toilet training approach trains your toddler more successfully than any arbitrary deadline.

Incidentally, even if a nursery school requires your toddler to be trained on entry, have no fear. Within a week, peer pressure will probably have him out of diapers, onto the potty, and buying Mickey Mouse underpants like every other three-year-old.

Bribes, Presents, and Hugs

I guess I'm a purist because I don't see why children should be rewarded with a present when they go to the potty. Gaining self-esteem should be enough of a gift.

However, many parents insist that their children would never be out of diapers if they hadn't given them those toys, packages of candy, or ice cream. I would recommend first showing your toddler how proud you are of his efforts with a hug; then, if you are convinced that only a reward will clinch the training, go ahead and give him one.

▼ ▼ ▼ ▼ ▼ ▼ ▼ ▼ ▼ ▼ ▼ ▼ ▼ ▼ ▼ ▼ ▼ ▼ ▼

What to Expect the First Few Weeks

1. Accidents on your best rugs, clothes, and furniture.

2. Alternative yeas and nays from your toddler about going to the potty (even with the most extravagant bribes).

3. Frantically searching for bathrooms whenever you and your toddler step outside the house.

4. Purchasing more pairs of underpants with flowers, dinosaurs, or balloons than you ever thought possible.

5. Endlessly questioning whether this really is the right time to toilet train or whether you are just being swayed by the opinions of friends and parents.

6. Looking at your watch constantly and trying to anticipate when your toddler will have to go.

7. Looking back with pride when your toddler finally slips away to the bathroom without even telling you.

◆ ◆ ◆ ◆ ◆ ◆ ◆ ◆ ◆ ◆ ◆ ◆ ◆ ◆ ◆ ◆ ◆ ◆

One Step Back:
Just When You Thought You Were Finished . . .

It could be a new sibling or baby-sitter, a big blowup between her parents, or simply a longing to return to the comforting days of diapers. Sometimes parents never learn why, but every toddler is bound to have days, weeks, and maybe even months when she seems to be having accidents constantly. (In the first few weeks of toilet training, count on at least a couple a day.) Toilet training is basically a dance of two steps forward, one step back.

When your toddler has a difficult period, try to figure out why. Disappointed and hassled as you may feel, getting angry at your toddler won't help him return to the potty.

Relax and believe in your child. A day will come when your toddler will suddenly go back to the potty without a care in the world.

Unless you are washing dozens of underpants daily for weeks on end or watching your rugs being destroyed by urine, I'd recommend not putting your toddler back in diapers. Instead, return to a gentle routine of helping your child to the potty every few hours or so.

▲ ▲

Tales of Success

Parents can easily find dozens of toilet training methods that guarantee success. But as the following stories illustrate, every child has her own style of becoming trained.

Wild Thing Rebecca's favorite words at age two and a half were "no" and "Don't do that." Her parents tried every game in the book to get her to use the potty. They kept her in underpants for three weeks, but then went back to diapers. They didn't have a washing machine in the apartment, and they said that everything reeked of urine during this training period.

Then her parents hit upon a plan. They bought a washing machine so that they wouldn't be unnerved by accidents. Then they devised a ritual. Every time Rebecca sat on the potty, they read her her favorite book, *Where the Wild Things Are*. Soon, her parents merely had to say the words "wild thing" and Rebecca was off to the potty. Toilet training became a fun experience.

You Call This a Vacation? Hannah's parents had diligently bought a potty when she was two years old. They also bought just about every adult and children's book on toilet training that was on the market. For two weeks, Hannah's mother took her to the potty before she left for work. Hannah seemed interested and easily urinated or had a bowel movement. Her mother expected that Hannah would soon be trained.

However, Hannah's baby-sitter didn't consistently take her to the potty during the day, partly because the parents had never stressed the importance of doing so. Then, because her schedule became so hectic, Hannah's mother stopped taking her to the potty in the morning. The next time her mother tried getting Hannah to the potty, Hannah started screaming, "I don't have to go!" Her mother tried bringing dolls, giving candy, making jokes, and even carrying Hannah to the potty. Finally, Hannah's parents gave up and decided to wait for the family vacation.

Before vacation her mother casually mentioned to Hannah that she would only wear big girl underpants when they were away. Both parents vowed to toilet train Hannah. On vacation they took Hannah to the potty religiously every two and half hours and, despite a large number of accidents, they didn't yield to diapers except at night.

Hannah's parents also resorted to some minor bribery such as having Hannah put a sticker on the potty every time she went. (For every six stickers Hannah got one new toy.) By the end of the three-week vacation, Hannah had acquired a stash of new toys and was totally trained.

No one will ever really know whether it was the stickers, the toys, or both parents being at their daughter's beck and call that trained Hannah. My gut feeling is that Hannah was trained because her parents worked together so consistently and adamantly.

My Big Brother Taught Me   Paul was almost three years old and still showed no interest in becoming toilet trained. He screamed bloody murder if his parents tried to get him on the potty or put him in underpants. Day after day he refused to wear anything but a ripped plaid shirt and blue jeans.

His parents were confused and decided to wait for signs of interest from Paul. His older brother, now five, had been trained when he was three. The two brothers shared the same room and spent a great deal of time together. When asked how Paul had crossed other milestones, the parents replied: "Don't ask us. Ask Alex, he's the parent."

Sure enough, one day when the parents were snooping by the boys' bathroom they found Alex sitting on the big toilet earnestly coaching Paul, who was on the potty. "You can do it. Don't worry, just keep on trying."

Over the next few days, Paul suddenly started wearing Alex's underpants. By the end of the week, Paul was basically toilet trained and had actually stopped wearing his blue jean uniform. Says the father: "Alex obviously has a different touch from ours. I don't know if he's more easygoing or whether it's peer pressure, but it works."

Oops, It Was an Accident   Steven and his father went off on an overnight jaunt to a small town in upstate New York. As he unpacked their bags, Steven's father suddenly had a panic attack. In his zealous effort to make sure that he had brought enough clothes to withstand every possible change in the weather, he had forgotten the most essential article, diapers. It was six o'clock and not a store was open on Main Street. What to do?

Two-and-a-half-year-old Steven had been going to the potty sporadically but was far from being trained. His parents admitted that they were ambivalent about training their son. Now there was no choice. Steven's father said with great sincerity: "I'm going to need your help. I forgot to bring diapers and all the stores are closed."

The result: Steven rose to the occasion. He used the toilet all that evening and all day Sunday. On Monday morning, Steven told his father that he wanted to buy underpants rather than diapers.

The reality of the situation forced the father to be definite and direct with Steven. For an ambivalent parent, running out of diapers may be the easiest way to train a toddler.

▼ ▼ ▼ ▼ ▼ ▼ ▼ ▼ ▼ ▼ ▼ ▼ ▼ ▼ ▼ ▼ ▼ ▼ ▼

Common Concerns

Q: If my toddler refuses to go to the potty, what should I do?

First of all, relax. Put some fun back into the situation and realize that this is just one more thing to which a toddler can say no. What's important is to allow your child the feeling that it's all right to disagree with you. Give your child as much dignity and leeway as possible.

You might try saying something like: "Oh, I see you don't want to go to the potty now. We'll go later." Then a few minutes later try again by saying, "Okay, it's potty time."

Remember, your toddler is allowed to refuse you. Just because he doesn't want to go to the potty now, doesn't mean that he won't want to go thirty seconds from now. Everyone eventually goes.

Q: When I take my child to the potty, why does she often say, "No pee pee," and then two seconds later urinate all over the floor?

By her behavior your child is saying, "I am still in charge of my pee." This is the action of a toddler declaring when, how, and where she is going to urinate.

If you are going to interpret incidents like these as unforgivable signs of hostility from the subordinate trooper and become very angry, it is all over for you. You have to be poker-faced and avoid becoming involved in a power struggle.

Try defusing the situation by saying something like: "Oh, I see you peed on the floor. You know where the pee goes. Next time how about going on the potty?"

Q: Why is my child, who seemed to have the hang of toilet training, suddenly having accidents?

The first step is to figure out if there is something at home that is creating stress. Has there been a recent change in your toddler's life? Are you or your partner spending less time with him? Have your in-laws been bothering you more lately? Does he have a new caregiver?

If something has changed, try addressing and relieving your toddler's worry. For example, if both parents have been away recently, say: "Daddy and Mommy have been so busy lately. We won't be traveling so much for a long time. We'll be spending more time with you."

A toddler is always reacting to his situation. It is important to be sensitive to his moods and patient with him. However, if your child is constantly having accidents, I would recommend taking him regularly to the toilet rather than putting him back in diapers. No matter what, your child will return to the potty.

Q: Why does my toddler refuse to make BMs in the potty?

Although experts say that toddlers gain control of their bowels before their bladder, most parents say that their toddler first urinates in the potty. The size, color, and plopping sound of bowel movements can be frightening.

A toddler who uses the toilet may worry that part of her body is disappearing when she hears her BMs being flushed away in a toilet. She may feel as if she is losing an essential and precious part of herself. Try reassuring your child by saying something like: "Your BM goes bye-bye. Nothing else goes away except your pee pee and BM."

Some children have frightening fantasies that the BM is attacking them when they feel the water splashing their bottoms. Again, reassure your toddler by saying something like: "BMs will never hurt you. It feels good to make BMs. Daddy and Mommy make them too."

Many parents are very anxious about their toddler becoming constipated. Remember, if you make too big a deal about BMs, your toddler may exert her power to withold. Of course, if your toddler seems to be continually constipated, check with your pediatrician to rule out the possibility of any medical problem.

Q: When should my child stop wearing diapers at night?

You may be surprised to find that night after night, week after week, your toddler remains dry. The control that a toilet-trained toddler achieves during the day often seems to creep into sleep.

However, I certainly don't consider it a failure if your toddler needs to wear diapers at night, and, if you are bothered by having to change the sheets, you should keep him in diapers at night. It's better for a toddler to wear diapers than to have to deal with a parent's anger or impatience.

To help keep your child dry at night you might try waking him and taking him to the potty before you go to sleep. Also, remember that your toddler is not a camel; he is bound to have wet sheets if he downs gallons of liquid before he goes to sleep. That's one of the problems with consuming night bottles.

Toddlers also may have more accidents if they have nightmares or if their sleep is very deep and relaxed.

Q: Can children really train themselves?

Parents never seem to forget the stories of children who toilet train themselves. "Just imagine," says one father enviously, "no screaming battles, no accidents in the middle of a car ride, no spending half your day escorting your kid to the toilet."

What I've found, however, is that children who "train themselves" are often trained by an older sibling. Parents can help their child train herself by picking up on the clues of readiness. But remember, you still have to help your toddler learn toileting even when she seems ready.

Q: Help! My child is three years old and shows no interest in being toilet trained.

Sometimes parents have to push development along because the outcome bears such great fruit for their child. I would recommend

SALLY'S POTTY PARTY

"Look! Jimmy is wearing Calvins©!"

that you start getting a three-year-old used to the potty by bringing him to it regularly. You want to give your toddler every opportunity to feel good about himself. Toilet training really will do that for a toddler. (Incidentally, your toddler probably has shown some signs of being ready, but they may have been too subtle to catch.)

Remember, toilet training should not be something you nag about. Don't make toilet training into a power struggle. Try making toilet training a process you share with your toddler, a fun experience to which he can't say no.

Summary

Toilet training can make parents feel inadequate and pressured. We worry about how to do it, when to do it, and whether our child will be the last one wearing diapers on the playground.

While you could spend the next decade reading the wealth of material on pees and poops, success in toilet training comes when parents feel they are doing the right thing by making their toddler more independent. Just as parents wean their child from the breast and from baby food, so parents help their toddler move from diapers to underpants.

It is important to make the toilet training process as relaxed and simple as possible. Bring out lots of substitute play materials, such as play dough and water. Let your toddler romp around the house naked. Forget about deadlines and privacy. Your toddler learns by watching. Your days of going to the bathroom alone are over.

Toilet training will give your child a new sense of self-esteem, self-control, and independence. But the path to using the potty won't be particularly enjoyable or relaxing. It is labor-intensive. Parents should expect many accidents, volatile moods, and plenty of "No's" when they remind their toddler to go.

▼ ▼ ▼ ▼ ▼ ▼ ▼ ▼ ▼ ▼ ▼ ▼ ▼ ▼ ▼ ▼ ▼ ▼ ▼

CHAPTER 8

When Parents Push Too Hard

'M GOING TO TELL YOU WHAT YOU PROBABLY ALREADY suspect: If you overschedule your toddler with too many formal classes, playdates, and educational experiences, your good intentions may very well backfire. Instead of making your toddler feel secure and competent, these structured minutes and hours may cause her to feel anxious and to tune out to the wonderful opportunities you've so carefully chosen. In thinking back to their own childhoods, most people remember activities they did freely and happily, not those they were forced into by well-meaning parents.

Yes, you want your toddler socialized and stimulated, but once again the key is moderation. I wouldn't recommend having your toddler sit in front of the television for five hours a day, but I also wouldn't recommend more than a few different classes per week or constant playdates. Although you may think this advice unnecessary, some children really do lead hectic lives. Says one mother: "I can't understand why my two-year-old daughter is becoming so whiny and spacey. After all, we are doing everything humanly possible to give her experience in the world and make her confident. Starting at nine in the morning I take her to gym class. Then at eleven o'clock we go to toddler painting class together. After that I often treat her to lunch at a great children's restaurant that supplies crayons and has Raffi music piped in through speakers. In the afternoon she takes a nap for an hour, and then at four o'clock off we go to a playgroup of eight mothers and their toddlers. On weekends, my husband and I take our daughter to cultural places, like museums and concerts. We love her so much we don't want her to miss anything."

In the name of love, parents sometimes take on the role of teacher in order to give their toddler a competitive edge. If you find that your style is "learn, learn, learn," then you are also pressuring your child. Do you rarely read your child a bedtime story without a little lecture on the ABCs? Do you rarely let your child run freely in the playground without first teaching her how to write her name with chalk on the pavement?

Pushing a toddler to learn before he is ready or interested won't help him to feel good about himself or about learning. Children are so tuned in to their parents that they can learn almost anything. But even when a toddler can count to forty, does she really understand the concept of numbers? For toddlers, the activity most appropriate to prepare them for reading, writing, and arithmetic is pure and simple play. Says one father: "I didn't realize how competitive I was about having the smartest toddler on the block until I was a parent. After all, I was my high school valedictorian and thought you had to start early! Suddenly I started getting obsessed about my son learning the alphabet by the age of three. Well, I did manage it. I tried to be casual, but in retrospect that was pretty much how I wanted to spend my free time with him. He was way ahead of every toddler I knew. But by the time he hit kindergarten, he shut down. He refused to look at a book. I think the whole experience with me teaching made him anxious and angry."

This chapter is a warning. Most toddlers don't get burned out. But it's important to be aware of what can happen in the name of parental love. It's wonderful for your toddler to have a day that combines a gym class and play at home, but remember, the key is balance.

▼ ▼ ▼ ▼ ▼ ▼ ▼ ▼ ▼ ▼ ▼ ▼ ▼ ▼ ▼ ▼ ▼ ▼ ▼
What Causes Toddler Burnout

1. Insisting that your toddler learn her ABCs, colors, and 123s in place of spontaneous, joyful play.

2. Teaching her the right way of playing with a toy instead of letting her figure it out through trial and error.

3. Taking your toddler to gym class in the morning and then on a playdate for the entire afternoon.

4. Giving him too much of a taste of the good life—movies, museums, the circus—before he's ready.

5. Overscheduling her day after day, week after week.

6. Making him feel that he isn't worth your love if he doesn't perform up to your standards.

▲ ▲ ▲ ▲ ▲ ▲ ▲ ▲ ▲ ▲ ▲ ▲ ▲ ▲ ▲ ▲ ▲ ▲ ▲

Why Parents Push

Parents overschedule their toddler for many reasons. Some are obvious. If you have a child whose large motor skills seem to lag, it stands to reason that you might enroll her in a gym class to catch up. If your toddler is shy, you might think that exposure to many people in many classes will help him outgrow his shyness. If your toddler has excessive energy, you might consider directed activities helpful. If your toddler isn't talking (which, by the way, many experts agree should not cause concern until a child is three years old), you might be inclined to talk too much or to overstimulate.

"Great! So I'll crayon you in for snack time on Tuesday."

Parents also overschedule their child because it satisfies their own needs. Are you pushing your toddler because an aspect of her personality is too close to yours for comfort? Are you overscheduling to make up for feeling deprived in your childhood? Are you overdoing because you worry that your child will lag behind when he gets out in the real world?

Remember, all these well-intentioned extracurricular activities can easily feel like stress to a toddler. A child feels pushed when her parents don't accept her for what she is—whether she's quiet, or energetic, or shy. The purpose of classes and playdates at this age is to socialize, rather than to learn actual skills.

Many working parents tell me that they send their child to formal classes as a way of having some control over his day. They say that it makes them feel better to know that their child isn't alone with one person and can get the benefit of being with an expert.

Two classes per week are probably fine for your toddler and won't overwhelm him. The problem is that if your toddler is exposed to too many children or too many experts in a week, he can feel unsettled and confused. This confusion can translate into his becoming too aggressive or too withdrawn.

▼ ▼ ▼ ▼ ▼ ▼ ▼ ▼ ▼ ▼ ▼ ▼ ▼ ▼ ▼ ▼ ▼ ▼ ▼

How to Tell If Your Child Is Burned Out

1. Your toddler, who used to be full of enthusiasm and excited about learning new things (even if it was taking apart the antique clock of your aunt's!), suddenly is not interested in what makes the world go round. Instead of playing and enjoying herself in playgroups, you notice her wandering around. Could her schedule of two new weekly playgroups be too much?

2. His whole conversation seems to consist of repeating what you have taught him, such as ABCs and counting. Maybe you have been too much the overzealous educator lately.

3. Your well-balanced, sociable child suddenly withdraws or becomes frenetic when she goes to friends' houses. Back-to-back playdates in the morning and afternoon could be doing her in.

4. Your toddler starts to cling, whine, and cry "I want to go home" whenever he is in a new environment. Too much of a new thing isn't a good thing for him.

You know your child best. If there are changes in her personality, you might consider whether she could be suffering from toddler burnout.

▲ ▲ ▲ ▲ ▲ ▲ ▲ ▲ ▲ ▲ ▲ ▲ ▲ ▲ ▲ ▲ ▲ ▲ ▲

What to Do If Your Toddler Is Burned Out

First, you need to look very carefully at your toddler's schedule. I'd recommend writing down a detailed list of your child's activities for the past week. Then examine it to see if he might be overscheduled. Does he have enough free time to do absolutely nothing? Can she dawdle, observe, and play at her own pace?

It's also important for parents to examine their own way of being with their child. Do you follow your child's lead instead of expecting him to do everything your way? Do you find yourself teaching her how to play with her toys rather than just being there for her, enjoying her excitement? Don't worry, she really will learn soon enough how to open her new cash register and ring its bells.

If you determine that your toddler is living on too tight a schedule, the next step is to cut back on his activities. You have to decide what benefits him most. It can take a great deal of courage for a parent to say, "Hey, this class (or playgroup) isn't for my child." But keep in mind that there are many years to come for your child to try out new experiences.

Also, if you think your toddler is happy for only the first hour of a two-hour class, take her home after one hour. There is no point in forcing a toddler to stick it out just because every other two-year-old in the class is staying. Or, if your toddler wants to play in the sandbox while all the other children are sitting quietly at circle time, why not let him do his own thing?

It doesn't mean very much if your child doesn't like a particular activity at this young age. I know one mother who told her daughter that if she didn't sit still during circle time at gym class she couldn't watch *Sesame Street* for a week.

▼ ▼ ▼ ▼ ▼ ▼ ▼ ▼ ▼ ▼ ▼ ▼ ▼ ▼ ▼ ▼ ▼ ▼ ▼

How to Avoid Toddler Burnout

1. Make sure your toddler has free time every day just to be by herself.

2. Remove him from a class in which the expectations of what a toddler can do are unrealistic. Despite what the teacher may say, or despite your own embarrassment, a toddler should not have to conform to rigid instructions.

3. Don't compare what your toddler can do to what all her friends do. Respect her uniqueness.

4. Remember, he has his whole life ahead of him for exploring and experiencing.

▲ ▲ ▲ ▲ ▲ ▲ ▲ ▲ ▲ ▲ ▲ ▲ ▲ ▲ ▲ ▲ ▲ ▲ ▲

Parent Burnout

Just as a toddler can burn out by being pressured, so can parents. If you are feeling too much responsibility to be the perfect parent and have the perfect child, it can take a great toll on your well-being.

Why do you need to be the perfect parent? Maybe you have found it difficult to be shy and quiet, so you don't want your child to go through this painful experience. Maybe you want to give your toddler a head start in school because you always felt so intimidated there. Or perhaps you feel that life is so cutthroat and competitive that you want your child to have every possible edge.

Therefore you push, schedule classes, and worry so much about your toddler that you become exhausted. The more you obsess, the more you can feel that everything you do as a parent is wrong and that something is very definitely wrong with your child.

Of course, most parents of toddlers are going to feel over-whelmed and worn out at one time or another. Children at this age are so mercurial and needy that their demands can trigger emotions in parents that may have been dormant or may never have been experienced. But if you find yourself feeling upset and discouraged about your toddler for any extended period of time, it's important to seek the advice of a counselor.

▼ ▼ ▼ ▼ ▼ ▼ ▼ ▼ ▼ ▼ ▼ ▼ ▼ ▼ ▼ ▼ ▼ ▼ ▼

When Burnout Hits You

1. Your sense of humor leaves you.

2. You count the minutes until your partner comes home from work and then go crazy because he or she is three-and-a-half minutes late.

3. You don't enjoy being with your child, even for a short time.

4. You blame yourself for all your child's flaws, and you worry constantly.

5. You have to keep working harder to stay involved with your child (and it's only ten o'clock in the morning).

6. Your partner comes home and offers to do something nice, yet nothing makes you happy.

7. You find yourself angry more often than usual.

8. Parenthood has become a chore.

▲ ▲ ▲ ▲ ▲ ▲ ▲ ▲ ▲ ▲ ▲ ▲ ▲ ▲ ▲ ▲ ▲ ▲ ▲

Summary

All parents want to give their children lifelong enjoyment and competency in such activities as dancing, swimming, reading, and drawing. However, forcing a toddler into an activity that is way beyond him, is guaranteed to turn him off. Why not allow the child to be the one to ask for the music and art lessons, to ask you to teach him how to bake and make play dough? You don't want to flood your toddler with so many opportunities at an early age that he feels as though nothing is his own idea.

When parents push their child too hard they also can take away her spontaneity and initiative. They may then find that they have to jump-start their child for almost everything she does. This vicious cycle between child and parent takes a toll on everyone's well-being. Let your toddler yearn. She will find activities for herself that she will love for the rest of her life.

▼ ▼ ▼ ▼ ▼ ▼ ▼ ▼ ▼ ▼ ▼ ▼ ▼ ▼ ▼ ▼ ▼ ▼

CHAPTER 9

The Firstborn Child

A FIRSTBORN CHILD IS LIKE A FIRST LOVE AFFAIR. THIS kind of unique love can't be repeated. Never again will you be so excited by the first step, the first sentence, the last bottle, the last diaper.

At the same time, being a first-time parent can be very anxiety provoking because it's a totally new experience. You may feel that you are on shaky ground because you don't know what to expect from your child, or, for that matter, from yourself. From morning till night you may feel that you are examining your firstborn through a microscope, interpreting his every smile, squeak, and interaction.

When you are new parents, it is almost impossible to keep from comparing your toddler to every other child on the playground. What if your child doesn't have a two-hundred-word vocabulary like some two-year-olds featured in child development books? What if it's true that if you do everything right for the first few years, your child will be confident for the rest of her life—but you've already made plenty of mistakes? You may feel as though your in-laws, parents, and friends are judging your every move.

First-time mothers and fathers may also find themselves confronting their own past history. For instance, if you were forced to eat for those starving orphans around the world, are you making your toddler finish every bite on his plate? If you were never allowed to raise your voice, are you totally unnerved when your toddler lets out an uninhibited scream? In addition to addressing your past history, you and your partner have to adjust to becoming a family and sharing time and feelings with your child.

All the attention and intensity of feeling firstborns receive from parents is a mixed blessing. On the one hand, the first child can seem mature beyond her years, winning the praise of every adult she meets for her good behavior and verbal precociousness. She almost can't help but take on the attitudes of her parents—responsible and directed toward success. But at the same time, all this seriousness can take a lot out of a child. He may try so hard to please that he loses sight of his own feelings and needs. For instance, is she learning the ABCs because she wants to or because it makes her parents proud? Is she drawing pictures becaue she loves to draw or because her parents love art? *Spontaneous* is rarely used to describe a firstborn child.

What makes being a first-time parent so difficult is that mothers and fathers, without meaning to, pressure their firstborn to represent the best in them. They have a hard time relaxing and accepting their child for who he is. Such pressure can make a toddler feel that he is a failure unless he lives up to his parents' expectations.

I've never met a parent who purposely makes his or her firstborn feel so much the center of attention that he can't break away from his parent's influence. Yet no matter how many children in a family have attended the Toddler Center, in parent groups parents always seem to talk about their beloved firstborn. One mother with a newborn said, only half in jest, "Sometimes I think I had a third child just so I wouldn't have the time to obsess and focus on my first." But she concluded, "Somehow I am managing to find the time."

▼ ▼ ▼ ▼ ▼ ▼ ▼ ▼ ▼ ▼ ▼ ▼ ▼ ▼ ▼ ▼ ▼ ▼ ▼

Traits of the Firstborn

Very few toddlers have all the traits described here, but you may see a few of them in your child if he happens to be the firstborn in your family.

1. Extremely verbal. Mother and father are in such constant verbal intercourse with the firstborn, asking her what color the sky is, if she likes strawberries, what flowers smell like, and so on, that she takes on the role of the great orator. Try to remember that silence is golden, and give her the chance to choose when to talk.

2. Gross motor skills lagging. "Wait for me," "Watch out!" "You're going to hurt yourself!" "Gasp, gasp," say the mother and father twenty-four hours a day. Rather than automatically putting your toddler in a stroller or carrying him, how about giving him a chance to exercise his own two legs?

3. More comfortable with adults than with peers. She is so much the center of Grandma's, Grandpa's, Aunt Sally's, Mom's, and Dad's universes that she's wary when faced with pint-size people her own age. Have her spend more time at the playground and don't make her the centerpiece of all your family gatherings.

4. Nonsharing. With all his relatives paying homage, how will your child learn to share his toys? Let him get used to the social graces of the toddler world by not interfering when someone takes his toys. Also, let him have the chance to reciprocate by taking toys from others.

5. Extremely empathetic. The firstborn becomes a consoling adult way before her time because she is so sensitive to and understanding of how her mother and father are feeling. It is better not to tell your toddler all the details of your emotional life and let her grow up on her own schedule.

6. Goal oriented. Your child may need constant approval for almost everything if the goals are yours rather than his.

7. Has difficulty adapting to new situations. First-time parents sometimes try to control their child's environment a little too much. If your child is always protected, he won't gain the experience of new situations that will later help him adapt.

8. Overcontrols emotions. With parents who always jump in before a whine grows into scream, a toddler is never given a chance to show anger, sadness, or hurt.

9. Lacks independence. If you always do for your toddler, he won't learn how to do for himself. When your toddler looks across the room to you for a visual check-in, don't assume he needs you to run over to him immediately. You can simply acknowledge him by staying seated and waving.

10. **Responsible citizen.** Firstborn children are often brought up to take life very seriously. Remember the motto: Work hard, play hard, and you'll have a more balanced citizen.

11. **Not a self-starter.** When the mother and father are the directors of the toddler film, always suggesting the next actions—what color paint to use, where to put the puzzle pieces, and so on—a child can come to rely on the input of others before making any move herself.

▲ ▲ ▲ ▲ ▲ ▲ ▲ ▲ ▲ ▲ ▲ ▲ ▲ ▲ ▲ ▲ ▲ ▲ ▲

Smothering in the Name of Love

There's no question that for first-time parents the most interesting thing in the whole world is their child. Without any other children around, the firstborn is by default always center, center, center. It may sound cynical, but if parents could only think of the firstborn as the third child of five, she wouldn't be under constant scrutiny and life would be much better for her.

Many mothers and fathers tell me that they feel they aren't good parents unless they are interacting and teaching every minute. First-time parents also may feel that if they don't protect their child with round-the-clock vigilance he really might not be able to protect himself or stay out of trouble.

Unfortunately, all this overinvolvement can backfire. For example, if you have always jumped in to make everything perfect, your child can feel that she isn't capable of doing things herself. When she gets upset because she has a little trouble fitting a piece in the puzzle, she will instantly ask for your help rather than spend the time to figure it out herself. She also can feel like a failure and full of shame because she can't live up to your, and her own, high expectations.

If you can sit back, relax, and observe what your child is doing, and acknowledge his actions with a nod of the head or a brief, quiet comment, such as, "Yes, good, you've done it," then you'd be giving

true support without pressuring your toddler. For example, our
teachers react to a toddler's painting by saying, "Oh, I see you made
a red painting," rather than, "That's the most gorgeous painting in
the world. What is it? Is it for Mommy or Daddy? Why don't you
put a little more green paint in it?"

It's easy to fall into the habit of overreacting in the name of love.
Considering the questions that follow may help you step back and
look at yourself as parents.

- Are you forcing your child to eat rather than merely pre-
  senting her with food and allowing her to take what she
  wants while you go about your business?

- Do you rock your child to sleep instead of letting him learn
  how to fall asleep alone?

- Do you rarely let your child cry, or do you allow her to experience some frustration and find ways to comfort herself?

- Do you seldom let your child wander more than two inches
  away, or do you keep a watchful eye from a (short) distance?

- Do you teach your child how to climb, jump, hop, or do
  you trust that she'll learn in his own good time?

- Do you push your child because your best friend's child
  puts the puzzle pieces into the right spot and knows her
  colors and letters? (DON'T!)

- Do you really believe that you have to play with your toddler every minute of the day, or do you let him play by
  himself and check in with you? When she calls out,
  "Mommy, I'm drawing with my crayons," can you stay
  seated and respond, simply, "Oh, I see you are drawing
  with your crayons"?

- Do you give your child a chance to be persistent and get a
  little frustrated before you jump in and help?

- Do you feel angry when another child takes your child's toy,
  or do you think, "Oh well, socialization has set in"? Do you

feel embarrassed when your child grabs all the toys from her playground gang, or do you think, "Oops, I guess she's experimenting with her newfound assertiveness"?

• Do you make a big fuss when your child gets a little scratch, or do you treat a little scratch with a little hug and a Band-Aid?

• Do you always rush to hug your child instead of giving him the chance to give the first hug? (Second and third children are often more cuddly because their parents don't always give the first hug and kiss.)

• Is your child predominantly demanding, impatient, and cranky? (Catering to her every wish can turn her into a little Napoleon.)

• Does your child become exceptionally demanding and angry when you pay attention to others? (How about trying out some of the old diversion techniques when you are talking on the phone? "I see you don't like me to talk to Aunt Tilly. Why don't you call your cousin on your play phone and I'll be off in a few minutes.")

• Do you often feel as though your firstborn is a rope around your neck? (Anyone would at times. Who wants to live with a prima donna 24 hours a day?)

Needing a Report Card

A lot of first-time parents tell me that they feel good when other people comment on how special their child is—so smart, so cute, so competent. They also tell me that they feel sad and angry when they hear any kind of criticism about their child.

Of course, most of us do care about other people's opinions. But if you need a constant report card from other people and take everything they say to heart, imagine the position you will put your child and self in! Says one mother: "My daughter always seems to be crying about something in her playgroup. If the cracker breaks in half, she cries. If she doesn't like the juice, she cries. If she doesn't get a certain toy, she cries. None of the other kids seem to be such criers. I feel so self-conscious, and I worry that every other parent thinks something is wrong with my daughter and with me as a mommy!"

If you frequently feel the need to ask the pediatrician, the babysitter, or your parents, if your child is all right, or if you constantly compare your child with others or feel embarrassed about your child's behavior, it may be that you don't think you are doing a competent job as a parent. Many first-time mothers and fathers in my parent groups have talked about these worries.

1. "I am always so concerned about my child's development, even though she can basically do what every other toddler does. I have never gotten over the fact that she was two months premature."

2. "I worry about my son not being popular much as my own father used to worry about me."

3. "I drive myself crazy needing to hear that my daughter is the smartest, prettiest, most articulate, because I am always comparing myself with my sister and her children."

4. "My marriage has been so difficult recently that I think the reason my husband and I have become so obsessed about our firstborn getting into the most selective nursery school is that it is one way of making us feel that we have succeeded at something."

5. "I cringe at my son's inability to come out from behind my skirt when he meets people."

Of course, every parent worries about how their child measures up in the outside world. You want to recognize and channel these worries so that they don't prevent you from being your toddler's most ardent supporter.

Giving Up Your Dreams

Parents may not often talk about their fantasies, but before a child is born, or perhaps even conceived, most of us create a vision of what that child will look like, how he or she will act, and whether the child will be a boy or girl. First-time parents, in particular, seem to have more intense expectations for their unborn child. Consider this mother's experience: "I dreamed that my first baby would be as brilliant as my great-grandmother, as funny as my brother, and as athletic as my best friend, who was always picked first for all the teams! Instead, I ended up with a boy who takes life very seriously, would rather point than talk, and to date hasn't shown any intellectual promise except to mix my expensive perfumes together."

Sometimes our dreams don't match the reality of what we get. Perhaps you wanted green eyes and you got brown; or you wanted a girl and you got a boy; or you wanted a bounce to every ounce and you got a placid child whose main interest in life seems to be eating; or you wanted your child to look exactly like you and instead she looks like your father-in-law.

After the first rush of happiness on learning that your baby is healthy, reality sets in. You may initially feel disappointed and even ashamed that your child doesn't match your fantasy. However, after a few weeks, most parents do adjust and delight in their baby as the most wonderful child in the world.

Reality may strike once again when your child becomes a toddler, and you may have to go through another period of giving up your fantasy. You may first have to mourn the loss of that sweet, helpless baby. Allow yourself these feelings so that you don't act out by hand-feeding your child or carrying him constantly instead of letting him walk. Next you have to take a look at who your two-year-old is. You may have wanted a well-behaved, agreeable boy, but instead you have a contrary wild man. You may have wanted a sociable, talkative girl, but instead you have a quiet, investigative researcher.

All these yearnings are normal and natural. But unless a parent can come to terms with reality and accept his or her toddler for what she is, a child's development can be hindered. Parents have to first acknowledge that their toddler doesn't fulfill their expecations in order finally to enjoy and appreciate her.

Summary

The love parents feel for their firstborn child can never be repeated. The first smile, the first step, the first words will never again be so exciting.

At the same time, being a new parent can be nerve-racking because it's an uncharted experience. Parents find themselves confronting their own past history. And, first-time parents often become wrapped up in seeing that their firstborn represents the best in them.

It's not surprising that the firstborn has some unique personality traits. She is often very verbal, extremely empathic, and goal oriented. He may be more comfortable with adults than with peers, and he may have difficulty adapting to new situations. The independence just isn't there.

Parents can draw from many ideas to help make their firstborn sturdier and more relaxed. Overinvolvement can backfire, making a child feel helpless rather than independent. Parents may have to give up their fantasies finally to appreciate their firstborn for who she is.

▼ ▼ ▼ ▼ ▼ ▼ ▼ ▼ ▼ ▼ ▼ ▼ ▼ ▼ ▼ ▼ ▼ ▼

CHAPTER 10

Your Toddler and the New Baby

When to Break the News

FOR MOST PARENTS, A SECOND PREGNANCY IS AN EXPERI-ence very unlike the first. After all, you are now sharing the nine months with your possessive and inquisitive toddler. Almost from day one of the pregnancy, many parents start thinking about when to tell their toddler, what to tell her, and how to get sibling life off to a good start.

Patterns for good sibling relationships start at the very beginning, *in utero*. My first suggestion: Don't tell your child too early about a new sibling. Since a toddler has very little sense of time, knowing about a new brother or sister six months before the arrival can feel like six decades of anxiety. In the best of all possible worlds, I'd put off telling your toddler about a pregnancy until the sixth or seventh month or until she keeps sliding off her mother's disappearing lap.

Unfortunately, most parents have to tell their toddler about the baby before he notices the bulge in his mother's stomach.

Strangers and relatives all love talking about pregnancy. Your toddler could easily feel confused if you don't acknowledge the baby when the whole world talks about her. One mother had to tell her two-year-old daughter in her fifth month because every time she walked down the street strangers asked when the baby was due. Another mother told her toddler before she had planned to because the doorman greeted them almost daily by saying, "I know it's a girl."

Try to follow your toddler's lead, answering only questions she asks. Toddlers seem to get the least anxious when parents don't give too many details about the new sibling. Parents often ask me how they should break the news about a new baby to their toddler. My feeling is that this first announcement should be low-key. Try simply describing the season: "We are going to have a new baby when it gets very hot and you don't have to wear a jacket."

Sometimes parents include their toddler in all the minute details of the pregnancy because they think it will bring the toddler closer to the new baby. Involving your toddler too much can backfire, however. For instance, one mother took her two-and-a-half-year-old on her visits to the gynecologist. One day the nurse pricked the mother's finger and drew blood. The two-and-a-half-year-old became very upset and didn't believe that her mother wasn't sick. For the next week the girl was more clingy than usual. She also kept saying: "Baby bad. She make Mommy sick."

I'm not saying that your two-year-old won't feel great joy on hearing the baby's heartbeat, but don't make the pregnancy the major news event of the day. Don't be surprised if your toddler picks up on his mother's mood swings of joy, anger, and exhaustion. Remember, when a mother is pregnant, her toddler emotionally feels as if he's pregnant as well. Your toddler might also feel at times as though he would like to climb back into his mother's womb. Many mothers say that their toddlers literally curl into a fetal position on their bulging stomach.

It's important that mothers don't overbook their calendar in the

"But it kicked me first!"

last month of their pregnancy. This is precious time that can be used to tune in to their toddler and give her extra attention. After all, one month from now she'll be sharing her mother with another sibling. In addition, a mother doesn't want to be so busy in this last period that she is exhausted before the new baby even arrives on the scene.

Many mothers say that they have twinges of regret and guilt during their pregnancy. They often feel sad and clingy with their toddler, particularly if he is the firstborn child. Their cozy relationship is soon going to change forever. Never again will it be just Mom and this one child. Says one mother: "The night I went into labor I just stood outside my first child's door crying as he slept. My husband kept saying: 'We have to go to the hospital. We have to hurry.' But I felt so sad that even the labor pains couldn't tear me away from my firstborn." Another mother recalls: "Here I was dilating very quickly, but I kept ignoring the pain. I was determined to finish the book I was reading to my daughter."

While it can be difficult to acknowledge the mixed emotions you may have about having another child, doing so will help you to begin to build a new picture of your evolving family. Gradually you can become the parent of more than one.

Preparing Your Toddler for the Birth

In the last month or so I'd recommend preparing your toddler for her mother's stay in the hospital and the baby's birth. Once again, try giving just the essential details, keeping the explanations low-key.

Showing your toddler photographs of herself as a newborn and telling the story of her birth can soothe her. "When you had grown big enough to come out of my stomach I went to the hospital with Daddy. The doctor said to us, 'Are you ready to have a baby?' We said yes. Then the doctor took Daddy and me into a room and you were born. We were so happy. We played with you and fed you in the hospital. Then very soon, Daddy, you, and I went home together."

You also might get your toddler involved in buying a few outfits for the baby and helping you pack your hospital bag. Try saying something like this: "I packed a little baby outfit for you to wear when I went to the hospital. I also packed a comb, nightgown, and toothbrush for me. This time you can help me pack the bag. This time I'll bring a picture of you, so the first thing the baby will see is you. Grandma is going to stay with you at our house when the baby is born. Daddy will bring you to visit the baby and me."

Many parents find it helpful to keep the newborn in the hospital nursery during their toddler's visit. This way the toddler can see the new baby but still get all of his mother and father's attention. One parent says she made her toddler's day by putting his photograph in the newborn's bassinet.

Many parents also sweeten the baby's arrival for their toddler by buying a surprise present. One three-year-old describes her visit to the hospital as the special day her mother gave her chewing gum. Another toddler remembers the baby's first day home as the day he got his rocking horse.

Getting Your Toddler on the Management Team

Giving your toddler a stake in the adult world can work wonders. It lessens her feelings of jealousy and also gives her more control. Let your toddler help bring diapers, powder the baby, sing to him when he cries. She will feel that she still has a place in the family and that this baby is truly hers. Almost like a first-time parent, the toddler can get an enormous sense of pride from her new brother or sister.

What About You—The New Mother

Even a toddler seems to get caught up in the great joy of a baby's arrival. It's almost as if *he's* given birth. After nine months of pregnancy, it is such a relief to see his mother calm, smiling, and proudly saying, "We have a baby for you." Be sure your toddler is there to greet you and the new baby when you return home from the hospital. Happiness is contagious. For many families the first few days with the new baby are a honeymoon.

But for how long? Some mothers quickly regain their energy, become focused, and function quite easily. These mothers are on a high, and nothing seems to faze them. Some mothers remain exhilarated for quite a while, but for many others hormones and exhaustion take over. At times a new mother may feel trapped and weepy, and anything her husband or children say may feel like a dagger.

Just as there is no easy way for a toddler to get used to a new sibling, a mother has to give herself time and permission to feel that she is a mother of more than one child. A family learns how to be a family. You have to learn how to be a parent of one, two, three, or more children.

If at all possible, get someone to help take care of you. The most important thing you can do for your toddler is to show her that you are being taken care of. Mood swings are particularly difficult for a toddler, who thinks that every blink of her parents' eyes are her doing.

Don't think that you have to do it all. You may feel that, because you managed alone with your first child, you should be able to do so with your second *now*—but you must realize that the experience is totally different this time around. One mother with teenage children still recalls the intensity of the first three months: "I can remember crying my eyes out sitting on the living-room floor surrounded by a screaming newborn and toddler. My husband came in from work to this pathetic picture and for a moment he said he truly thought I had lost it. Competent, creative, sturdy me, who had worked ten hours daily as a journalist, needed more help. True, I had found the first few months with my first child hard, but in retrospect it was nothing compared to mothering two. I just felt totally overwhelmed and wondered how I would get through the experience."

Get as much help as you can, and don't feel guilty. Send out for dinner, hire a housecleaner, send clothes to the laundry, have your partner take vacation (though it won't be one), hire someone to coo at the newborn or to run wild with the toddler. You will help your toddler if you get help, because you will be much more giving with him. The situation might also provide the opportunity for your toddler to form a close relationship with someone else. For example, one father says that his three-year-old daughter developed a wonderful relationship with her grandparents. Until the baby was born, the grandparents had never spent time alone with their granddaughter. Now, the grandparents take her to their house for dinner once a week.

▼ ▼ ▼ ▼ ▼ ▼ ▼ ▼ ▼ ▼ ▼ ▼ ▼ ▼ ▼ ▼ ▼ ▼ ▼

How to Keep Your Toddler Feeling Good with a New Baby

1. Give him special privileges and big kid time alone with you.

2. Ask your toddler's advice on baby care. "What should we do to get this baby to stop crying? Do you think he's hungry?"

3. Let her help take care of the baby when she wants to.

4. Just like old times, have the three of you—Mom, Dad, and your toddler—go out for lunch, take a walk, and so on.

5. Accept your toddler's feelings about the new baby—hate, jealousy, or anger.

6. Don't push your toddler to grow up. This is not the time to try to get her off bottles, out of diapers, or into a bed.

▲ ▲ ▲ ▲ ▲ ▲ ▲ ▲ ▲ ▲ ▲ ▲ ▲ ▲ ▲ ▲ ▲ ▲ ▲

Will Life Ever Be Back to Normal?

Try to let life continue on as normal a schedule as possible for your toddler. Regularity is the most important way to help your toddler adjust to the new baby. Put him to sleep at the same time, have dinner at the usual hour. If he goes to a playgroup don't let him miss it. In fact, as long as your toddler doesn't seem to feel excluded, you might step up the number of playdates to keep him busy in his own, baby-free world.

Of course, you don't want to make it appear that this new baby is other than a wonderful prize, either. Don't say no to visitors just because you are afraid that your toddler will feel rejected. (Do say no, however, if you find visitors too exhausting.)

Fortunately, most people are sensitive to the feelings of older children. But your toddler is still bound to feel some hurt and rejection when visitors "ooh" and "ah" (no matter how discreetly) over the new baby. Before the hordes of baby admirers descend on your house, it will help to prepare your toddler. Try saying something like: "When you were a baby everyone came to see you. Today you can show your new baby to Uncle John."

Making your toddler feel a part of the grown-up crowd can give her a big boost. Let her pass out cookies and give a tour of the baby's room. Most people will bring presents for your toddler as well as for the baby. Let your toddler open both presents. But if your eighty-eight-year-old aunt arrives with hand-knit booties just for the baby, your toddler will probably be satisfied with just opening and examining the present.

Bring Back the Bottles

Immediately after the baby's birth your toddler may regress by asking for a bottle or suddenly needing to wear diapers again. My advice: Go with the flow. You're not going to destroy your toddler's development by letting him have a bottle once in a while. (I wouldn't ask him if he wants a bottle like the baby, but I wouldn't refuse to give him one if he asks.)

Don't go overboard with the familiar homily, "You are the big girl (or boy) now." You will see that your toddler often feels like a baby and wants to be treated like one, too. When your toddler takes to the floor on all fours, try acknowledging these feelings. "Sometimes you want to be a baby, sometimes you don't. I love you any old way."

Again, this is not the time to push your toddler to grow up. I wouldn't try getting her off bottles or out of diapers in the first few months of the baby's life. If you want to move your toddler out of her crib, plan to do it a few months before the baby comes.

How Much to "Ooh" and "Ah"

A perfect time to coo and snuggle with your adorable newborn is when you change his diapers. After all, isn't this the easiest and most natural time to be lovey-dovey with your baby? (Particularly now that he is on the changing table, about two feet higher than your toddler!)

Sometimes your toddler will watch joyfully, other times she will be in a jealous rage. While it can be difficult for a two-year-old to see her parents kissing the new baby, you don't want to show the baby your love only at the 2 A.M. feeding. It is also important for your toddler to see (though not twenty-four hours a day) that you do love the baby and respond to his needs. A toddler can become insecure about her parents' love for her if she never sees them loving her siblings.

How to Include the Toddler

You might be surprised at the growth experience the new baby can provide for your toddler if you can figure out creative ways to include and have special time for him.

When you are nursing or feeding the baby, you might get your toddler to tell the baby a story or sing him a song. You might try feeding the baby on a couch that is big enough to hold everyone. When a baby is nursing, all that good milk may inspire a toddler to ask for a nip himself. If you are comfortable with the idea, let your toddler take a turn. Breast milk comes out more slowly than liquid from a cup, and it is less creamy than cow's milk. It is doubtful that your toddler will ever ask for his mother's milk again.

Of course, if you feel awkward about letting your toddler try a sip, don't do it. Try explaining: "This is baby milk. You drink grown-up milk and other things like juice that are just for big children, not for babies."

When the baby is screaming, how about asking your toddler for advice: "What do you think we should do to quiet this baby?" Sometimes a two-year-old's "Hush" really does work better than a mother's touch, and even if it doesn't you will make your older child feel needed. In conspiratorial whispers you can also bring your toddler to your side by saying, "Boy, sometimes the crying can really get on your nerves."

You need to let your toddler know that you will still have special time alone for her. Articulating your plans, slight as they may be, is very reassuring. You might say, for example, "As soon as the baby goes to sleep I will play just with you," or "As soon as I finish changing the baby's diaper I'll go out just with you to the grocery store."

Toddlers get a feeling of specialness when you let them know that they have big kid privileges. For instance, if you take your toddler to an ice cream parlor, try saying, "Babies can't have ice cream or cake, only big kids like you can."

I can still picture the smile of understanding that lit up the face of one of the children at the Toddler Center one day. This twenty-eight-month-old boy had a new baby and was constantly pouncing on the other children in the class. I said casually one day: "Andy, this is just your room. Alice can't come here. This school isn't for little babies." Andy suddenly realized that he didn't have to try so hard to protect his turf because his sister would never be allowed on it. He relaxed, flooded with relief, and began to play peacefully again.

News Report of the Hour

Whatever is happening in your household should usually be reported to the toddler. Toddlers have inner antennae, and they believe they are the cause of everything from illness to grumpiness. It helps to explain and then reassure that most things in the family have nothing to do with them. For example, if the baby runs a fever and the parents haven't slept all night, now is the time to say: "Mommy and Daddy are feeling a little tired today because the baby is a little sick. No one makes anyone sick. You didn't make the baby sick."

Time Alone: How Much?

Your toddler will feel more accepting of the baby if you can give him some time alone. Ironically, after being with a wailing newborn, parents may even find it relaxing to be with a toddler. This separate time is often most pleasant if you take your toddler out of the house, away from the baby. Different children like to do different things alone with their parents. One toddler might like taking a walk, another might like going on a playdate without the baby. Half an hour a day alone can work wonders.

But remember, you'll never be able to divide yourself equally between your children. You will quickly burn out if every part of your day is spent rushing between alone time with your baby and alone time with your toddler. Impossible as it may seem, try to keep your needs in mind, too.

Some parents go overboard in trying to make their toddler feel that life has not changed one iota. Says one mother: "Everyone kept telling me that as long as someone holds and feeds the baby she'll be fine. They said it's more important to concentrate on my son. So I spent the day trying to make my toddler feel he was still in a way my only child." This isn't good for either the toddler or the baby. If you are constantly leaving the baby to spend time alone with the toddler, you are giving the message that there is something wrong about the whole family being together. The children will also be deprived of the opportunity to form an early relationship or to learn to be flexible.

Recognizing Your Toddler's Feelings

Your toddler is going to have passionate and turbulent emotions toward you, the baby, and just about every human being she comes in contact with. You can't ignore the feeings your toddler will have of being displaced by this tiny intruder. Painful as it is, your toddler is going to feel squeezed out.

You have to allow these feelings of hatred, jealousy, and rage. At the same time, of course, your toddler will have feelings of love and pride and will share in the happiness of having a new family member. It is extremely important to let your child know that he can have any thoughts he wants and that you will still love him. You don't want your toddler to grow up feeling bad about having "bad" feelings. Your toddler needs to know that bad feelings won't destroy his parents or him.

When your toddler stalks away from you and slams her bedroom door, try saying something like, "Even when you are angry at Mommy, she still loves you." When your toddler screams "I hate you" at the baby, lightly say: "Sometimes you like your sister, sometimes you don't. You seem to be having a hard time because I'm feeding her rather than playing with you."

At the Toddler Center we often use the words "sometimes you do . . . sometimes you don't . . ." to clarify the children's feelings. Letting toddlers know that their feelings can change helps them to be less afraid of their "bad" feelings.

Difficult as it is, don't become too involved in your toddler's anger. Keep your reactions light and friendly. For instance, one two-year-old was constantly hitting her caregiver after her baby brother came on the scene. This caregiver had been taking care of the little girl five days a week for over a year. The caregiver decided not to take the hitting seriously and to give the toddler extra doses of attention. The caregiver playfully defused the situation by explaining the two-year-old's feelings. "So, you are angry and want to fight? Put up your dukes! I still love you even when I hold the baby." Hearing these words greatly calmed the toddler.

Keep at it. Your toddler hears you even though he may not act rationally. Changes almost always bring on a flood of new emotions for your toddler. Eventually your articulations of his feelings will sink in, and he will feel relieved that someone understands him even when he often doesn't understand himself.

▼ ▼ ▼ ▼ ▼ ▼ ▼ ▼ ▼ ▼ ▼ ▼ ▼ ▼ ▼ ▼ ▼ ▼
How to Tell If Your Toddler Feels Left Out

You can expect some or all of these behaviors to occur when your toddler has a new sibling. These behaviors are signs that your toddler would benefit from some extra attention from you.

1. Has more temper tantrums.

2. Wants to stay close to her mother's or father's side almost all the time.

3. Has sleep problems.

4. Is angry almost all the time.

5. Is too good.

6. Cries over almost everything.

7. Eats constantly or hardly at all.

8. Rarely wants to play with anyone.

9. Regresses: uses baby talk, refuses to dress himself, stops using the toilet.

▲ ▲ ▲ ▲ ▲ ▲ ▲ ▲ ▲ ▲ ▲ ▲ ▲ ▲ ▲ ▲ ▲ ▲ ▲

Jealousy

No matter how diligent or saintly the parents, a child is bound to feel jealous of a sibling. Jealousy, like love, is part of the range of human emotions. Until now, you may not have seen your toddler truly jealous because she may never have been in such an intense competition to win her parents' love. It can be pretty scary watching your toddler show intense, hard-driving jealousy for the first time. She may throw herself on the floor, convulsing with heart-wrenching sobs, the very moment the new baby wants to nurse.

A toddler's jealousy of a sibling can be subtle or dramatic. You might find your toddler suddenly lashing out at you, saying things like, "The baby hates you." Or your once active toddler may seem unusually withdrawn and quiet. Try reassuring your toddler by repeating calming thoughts, for example, "Even when Daddy holds the baby he still loves you. I see that the baby really bothers you today. Let's you and I have a hug."

Jealousy has no time limit. Your toddler can seem happy until the baby starts to upstage him with cuteness or reaches a new milestone, such as crawling, sitting up, or walking. Your toddler might then start to suck his thumb, twirl his hair, or refuse to get dressed or to sit on the potty. During these times, give your toddler extra attention and extra hugs.

If a parent really is partial to one child, then the toddler may experience feelings of extreme jealousy. Many parents are caught by surprise when they find that even their middle child, often the family negotiator, is jealous of a new baby. Here's what happened to one middle child: "We never worried about Sara. However, a year after her brother was born, Sara, at three years of age, began to have intense temper tantrums. We realized that part of the reason she was so jealous was that once again she had to share us. We had sort of forgotten her because she was always so easy. But when we finally focused on her, she was calculating everything her siblings now got, down to the last raisin."

▼ ▼ ▼ ▼ ▼ ▼ ▼ ▼ ▼ ▼ ▼ ▼ ▼ ▼ ▼ ▼ ▼ ▼

Helpful Baby Talk for Toddlers

1. Accept his feelings

Toddler: "I hate the baby."

Parent: "Sometimes you like your brother, sometimes you don't."

2. Give special time

Toddler: "I want you."

Parent: "As soon as I finish feeding the baby, I'll play just with you."

3. Give special privileges

Toddler: "Is the baby coming with us?"

Parent: "Babies can't have ice cream and pizza. Only big kids like you can."

4. Let your toddler know you love her

Toddler: "I'm going to hit you."

Parent: "Even when I hold the baby I still love you. I know it's hard because you want me to yourself."

▲ ▲ ▲ ▲ ▲ ▲ ▲ ▲ ▲ ▲ ▲ ▲ ▲ ▲ ▲ ▲ ▲ ▲ ▲ ▲

▼ ▼ ▼ ▼ ▼ ▼ ▼ ▼ ▼ ▼ ▼ ▼ ▼ ▼ ▼ ▼ ▼ ▼ ▼ ▼

Common Concerns

Q: No matter where I go, everyone always focuses on the baby, saying he's so adorable. What should I say to my toddler?

Although you might wish that all this attention would go away, you have to acknowledge it. But you want to let your toddler know that you are sensitive to her feelings. I would try saying: "Everyone seems to love babies. When you were this small everyone would run over to you and say the same things."

If your toddler seems particularly jealous when the baby gets a large dose of attention, spend some time alone with her. Her nose may be a little out of joint, but, if you make her feel the center of your universe, it won't stay that way for long.

Q: Ever since the baby was born my son refuses to go to his playgroup. Should I make him go?

Does he not want to go to his playgroup because you are staying home with the baby? I suggest that you take him to his playgroup, even if you have to bring the baby with you, because it is so important not to disrupt your toddler's schedule.

Q: I'm worried that if I tell my toddler that the baby is sleeping in our room he'll want to move in.

There is no question about it, your toddler will feel jealous and probably will want to camp out in your room if the baby is there. A good compromise that would still allow you quick access to your newborn might be putting the baby in the hallway right next to your room.

By the way, if you sneak the baby into your room, your toddler will definitely find out. Every child's radar goes up with the arrival of a new sibling.

Q: Whenever I nurse the baby, my daughter jumps into my lap. It's driving me crazy.

This is the time when you need to be mother octopus. Have a book ready for her to read, a story in your head, or some crayons to keep her busy until the baby has finished nursing. It also helps to let your toddler know that you'll give her special time when you are done. "As soon as the baby finishes eating, I'll put him to sleep and have special time just with you."

Q: It makes me so angry that people keep saying to my two-year-old, "Now you are going to have to be Mommy and Daddy's big boy."

I would make it clear to your two-year-old that you want him to be your two-year-old. When people throw your son the familiar big boy line, how about saying: "He'll always be my firstborn. That means he'll always be older than the baby. But that also means he can feel very big or very little. I'll love him any way."

Q: I recently had a cesarian and can't give that much attention, particularly physical, to my daughter.

First of all, let your child know that you'll soon be up and about. In the meantime, make sure your partner does his share of rough-and-tumble with your toddler. But remember, your presence is what is really important to your child. She just needs to feel that you still delight in her even with a new baby. Sharing in some quiet activities, such as reading or drawing, will make her feel that you are there for her.

Summary

When a mother is pregnant, a toddler often feels as if she is pregnant. Expect your child to pick up on her mother's moods of joy, anxiety, and exhaustion. You also may feel both guilty and ecstatic about giving your firstborn a sibling.

Make the pregnancy as relaxed as possible for your toddler. Since a two-year-old has no sense of time, put off telling him about the new baby until he can no longer fit on his mother's lap. When you finally do tell your child about the new baby don't make the pregnancy the major topic of the day. Take your toddler's lead, answering only questions he asks. Explain the birth and hospital stay in a simple, low-key style.

Once the baby arrives, it helps to keep your older child's life on schedule. Giving your toddler a stake in the adult world by letting her care for the baby and by spending special time with her will help her feel that she still has a place in the family.

But no matter how conscientious you are, your toddler is going to feel squeezed out and have turbulent emotions. You need to allow these feelings of jealousy and anger. You can also help your toddler understand his feelings by articulating them for him.

Be kind to yourself. Remember, you have to learn how to be a family. Parents have to give themselves time and permission to adjust to being parents of more than one child.

▼ ▼ ▼ ▼ ▼ ▼ ▼ ▼ ▼ ▼ ▼ ▼ ▼ ▼ ▼ ▼ ▼ ▼ ▼

CHAPTER 11

Sibling Relationships

MPOSSIBLE AS IT MAY SEEM, ONE DAY YOUR TODDLER MAY actually be grateful for her brother or sister. I truly believe that the greatest gift a parent can give a child is a sibling. Long after parents are gone, brothers and sisters will be there for each other. Like no one else in the world, siblings can reminisce and understand each other because they share a common childhood.

Sisters and brothers also give each other a dress rehearsal in the ways of the real world. They teach each other how to fight and compete. But the question is, of course, how do you get your children to love and cooperate with each other? After all, isn't a warm, growing relationship what all parents want for their sons and daughters?

At the Toddler Center we have developed strategies for parents that help bring siblings close to each other. Many of these ideas can also be used to help your toddlers in their relationships with friends.

Don't Jump In

In a nutshell: Stay out of your children's relationships. After years of observing siblings, the late Dr. Frances Fuchs Schacter, the first director of the Toddler Center, concluded that children gain confidence and a sense of comradery when adults leave them alone to establish their own friendships.

Difficult as it may be, particularly when your children come screaming to you in tears, let them fight it out and express such negative feelings as anger, jealousy, and hostility peppered with hatred. Once parents step between their children and become the judge of sibling fights and feelings, what may have been just a brotherly or sisterly squabble quickly escalates into a battle of life and death.

Why? What all siblings are really fighting about is their mother's and father's love. No child wants to share her parents. Think back to your own childhood. Didn't you often fantasize on the joys of life as an only child? Become a meddler, and jealousy between children usually worsens.

True, adults may get a bit of peace and quiet when they intervene, but it's only a temporary solution. Your children will stay angry at each other and most definitely at you. In fact, you will have set the stage for the next battle by becoming the judge. The child whom you defend may become more of a crybaby, and the one whom you reprimand may become more of a bully. I've seen over and over that the less parents regularly interfere, the less children really hurt each other.

This is not to say that siblings won't scream, scratch, pinch, and bite when left to their own resources. But in the end they usually make up on their own terms (they also don't seem to hit each other quite so hard). They figure out how to negotiate and maybe even compromise. One father reports: "Mark and Julie were having one of their constant fights. Julie slyly approached Mark and bit him solidly on his back. Mark instantly cried out: 'Daddy, Mommy, you have to help me. Make Julie stop.' I felt so humiliated for Mark that here he was five years old and he was calling out for us to help him fend off a two-year-old. For once I decided to stay out and said as calmly as I could through clenched teeth: 'Mark, sounds like you are angry. I know you can handle this.' A few minutes later, the victorious Julie returned to Mark for round two. For almost the first time in his life, docile Mark shoved her away and yelled, 'Get away from me!' Julie was stunned, and this time it was her turn to cry. Very soon they started to play again with great gusto. The next day Mark continued to be proud that he had finally stood up to his bullying baby sister."

Parents have to work really hard to stay mum. The bickering and spitefulness can drive even the most patient mother and father crazy. Parents also have to believe that their children are sturdy enough to handle the fights and bad feelings. Children gain an incredible sense of self-esteem when they feel that their parents trust them to work out relationships. In the jargon of the nineties, empower your sons and daughters by butting out.

Of course, it is a lot easier not to interfere if your children are over the age of two. But can a parent really sit back and leave a sweet, defenseless one-year-old baby at the mercy of his aggressive two-and-a-half-year-old sister? Yes, I think so. In fact, as soon as you think that the baby can withstand a poke or two, try to get in the habit of not intruding. When you see your two-and-a-half-year-old walk by the baby and "accidentally" give him a push, don't make a federal case out of the aggression. Try to ignore as much as you possibly can. A pinch and a little messing around with a chubby one-year-old can be tolerated. (Obviously, in the baby's early months you will have to be more of a guard.)

Staying out of your children's relationship doesn't mean that you ignore their feelings. Your children are going to have stormy emotions toward each other. Children need to know that their bad feelings won't hurt anyone. For instance, when your two-year-old comes running to you in tears because his six-year-old sister grabbed his favorite Big Bird doll, try saying sympathetically: "You are so upset with Molly. Tell Molly that's your Big Bird."

Try a similar approach when the six-year-old screams that the two-year-old messed up her dress-up box: "Oh, I'm really sorry. I know just how you feel. He gets into my stuff too." Then, with a knowing wink, add, "I trust you can handle this."

It's amazing how a simple confirmation of emotions can defuse a potentially gigantic blowup. When you see your toddler looking as if she's ready to pounce on your newborn, take a deep breath, put your healing hands on her shoulder, and say compassionately: "Claire, I can't let you hurt the baby and nobody will hurt you. I see that it gets you very angry when I am taking care of him and can't play with you." This type of verbal understanding is like a balm for soothing raw aggression.

▼ ▼ ▼ ▼ ▼ ▼ ▼ ▼ ▼ ▼ ▼ ▼ ▼ ▼ ▼ ▼ ▼ ▼ ▼

The Five Commandments for Raising Loving Siblings

1. Stay out of your children's fights.

2. Articulate your children's feelings without adding or subtracting to them.

3. Give each child some time alone with you.

4. Give each child the love he needs by looking at him as an individual.

5. Remember the boundaries: Children on one side and parents on the other.

▲ ▲ ▲ ▲ ▲ ▲ ▲ ▲ ▲ ▲ ▲ ▲ ▲ ▲ ▲ ▲ ▲ ▲ ▲

Your Children Won't Kill Each Other

Parents can't be expected to do the impossible, sit back while their children fight to kill. While I believe that parents should refrain from meddling in sibling fights at almost all costs, there have to be some rules for safety and sanity. Every family has to determine its own rules of acceptable behavior. (For example, many parents don't allow hitting with objects.)

Family rules and consequences should be clearly known. Your toddler then has the power to either follow the rules or accept the consequences. For example, perhaps anyone who bites gets time out in her room.

One of Life's Painful Situations

Parents often seem to feel less anxious about their children's relationships if they accept that at times having a sibling is just going to be one of life's painful situations for a child. Every child is going to go through periods of stress and rejection because of a brother or sister. Nothing parents can say about the benefits of a cooing baby or an accomplished older sibling is going to make their toddler feel totally happy and accepting.

Favoritism or Equality?

It really is impossible to treat siblings equally. Every child will have different feelings and difficulties at different points in his life. Good, sensitive parenting means giving each child what he needs. To do so a parent must assess each situation for each child.

Treating each child differently can be hard for many parents. Most of us have been brought up to believe that if we don't give identically we are playing favorites. Consider the lengths to which one mother went: "My two boys used to watch *Sesame Street* together. Naturally they both wanted to sit on the same side of the couch. My solution to their seating arrangement was to put on a timer so that they switched positions every five minutes." Now this mother recollects: "I thought they would become better friends because I was treating them the same, but they actually became more involved in who got what. The dividing of the couch become symbolic of their relationship. They began to fight over everything. To this day I also get a headache when I hear a kitchen timer go off."

Parents often tell me that the concepts of equality and favoritism are even more complicated because in their heart of hearts they don't feel the same about each child. One father explains his preferences for his older son: "We are much more alike. He is diplomatic and well liked. On the other hand, my younger son does all kinds of things I'm afraid to do. He's funnier and more creative than I."

Often it helps to look inward. No matter how much we might wish to erase our own past histories and preferences, we can't. Why are our feelings stronger for one child stronger than those for the other? Were you, the firstborn, always jealous of the second child? Were you labeled the impossible brat or the brilliant saint who could do no wrong? Were you the protected baby?

How do you know if you are favoring one child over another? Take a step back and you'll probably see that you feel passionately sympathetic for your favored child in a sibling fight. One father explains how he was reliving the old battles of his childhood: "I so much identified with my youngest son that in the midst of their fight I would call my older son by the name of my brother, who fought with me constantly."

Parents often overreact in helping the child they identify with the most. For instance, if you are a firstborn still fighting the fight against your younger sibling, you might be too protective of the older child. One mother reports that she was often on the side of her oldest daughter because as a child her mother had always defended the baby, not her. "I was having these intense emotions, disproportionate to the situations, feeling old, unresolved angers. My younger child's feelings were badly hurt; she felt abandoned. She couldn't understand why I always jumped to her sister's defense."

It can be helpful to remember, especially when you feel much more connected to one child, that your feelings about each of your children will constantly change and grow. The child you identify with the most today will not necessarily be the child you feel most strongly about tomorrow.

Individualize

If your toddler is the kind of child who doesn't readily participate and is often fearful, try not to go overboard when he shows aggression toward a sibling. You may almost want to shout "Bravo" when this child finally teases, pushes, or verbalizes that he doesn't like his brother or sister. But since the behavior of the civilized world prevents you from congratulating him, simply report on his feelings. After he throws all his brother's toys on the floor, how about saying, "I see you got very angry when your brother took your book."

On the other hand, if you have a child with a hot, passionate temperament, you'll have to maintain a more careful vigil, especially around the baby. You might also set a few more ground rules, such as no kicking and no throwing toys.

▼ ▼ ▼ ▼ ▼ ▼ ▼ ▼ ▼ ▼ ▼ ▼ ▼ ▼ ▼ ▼ ▼ ▼ ▼

Reassuring Without Interfering

1. Instead of: "Why can't you two play nicely? Now, you two share and no more screaming."

Try: "Sounds like you are pretty angry at each other. Maybe you need some time alone so you can each play with separate toys."

2. Instead of: "You are the big brother, you should know better."

Try: "I can't let you hurt the baby and nobody will hurt you. I see it can make you angry when I'm feeding your sister. As soon as I am finished I'll play just with you."

3. Instead of: "Your sister is a bully. I'm going to get your toy back for you."

Try: "Boy, that can make you angry when someone takes your toy. Tell your sister you want it back. I know you can do it."

4. Instead of: "Can't you see I'm bathing your sister? I can't play with you all the time."

Try: "As soon as I finish with this bath I'll be alone just with you. Now let me give you a hug."

5. Instead of: "You are the older one. There is going to be no TV or dessert unless you let your brother play with your pocketbook."

Try: "I know just how you feel. He likes to take my pocketbook too. I know you can handle this."

▲ ▲ ▲ ▲ ▲ ▲ ▲ ▲ ▲ ▲ ▲ ▲ ▲ ▲ ▲ ▲ ▲ ▲

Playdates: They're Not Playing with Me

Children should be allowed to have their own friends. When one child has a friend at the house, I would generally try to let that be her own playdate. Have your children understand that they get time alone with their friends.

Your toddler will inevitably come running to you when her older sister and friends slam the door in her face. Be empathic and let her vent her feelings. And be prepared to do something with her yourself. Your older child shouldn't have to be the baby-sitter for your toddler.

Also, don't be surprised when your toddler comes running to your side because his own friends drop him for the company of his accomplished, sophisticated, five-year-old brother. I don't think you should expect your two-and-a-half-year-old to win his friends back. Instead, try saying to the older child: "This is not your playdate. Now, how about you making that bridge with these blocks?"

Tips and Tales

Stepping in Their Shoes   Seven-year-old David seemed to spend most of his free time picking on his three-year-old sister, Ali. Hitting and crying were the activities of the afternoon for the two siblings. It was hard for Ali to stand up to David, and she rushed to her parents the moment the battles became intense.

Her parents saw that Ali longed for the day when David would include and treat her as a friend. One afternoon, the father said to Ali and David: "You know, I was a lot like Ali when I was small. My brother, Uncle Roger, used to really take things out on me. I thought he hated me all the time. But guess what? Today we are best friends. And you know what, Ali, you are a lot tougher than I was. I used to run away before my brother even caught me."

The story seemed to click with the brother and sister. They could see that they might actually become friends. Ali also felt empowered knowing that her father had felt even more timid than she.

Tip: Children feel relieved when they can see that their parents really understand how they feel. Telling a toddler "When I was your age" stories often helps your child feel stronger and more understood.

One Day a Coward, the Next Day a Lion   Twenty-six-month-old Kate would approach her eleven-month-old brother, Oliver, with a big, satisfied grin, as if she was going to hug him. However, instead of a cuddle, Oliver got a pinch. Often he burst into tears at the sound of his big sister's voice. He was conditioned to be afraid of her. Everyone called Oliver "the little coward." Oliver's parents were convinced that he was going to be the wimp in the family, the child everyone picked on. However, they decided that they would not interfere too much, punish Kate, or make her feel like the "bad" child. (They did keep a close watch and remove the baby whenever Kate's aggression escalated.)

Guess what? By about the age of one Oliver started to feel more powerful and began to keep up with his two older sisters. By the age of eighteen months he often intimidated them. He grabbed their toys and wouldn't let go no matter how hard they chased him or how far they dragged him across the floor.

The latest report from these parents is that the oldest daughter, Vicky, who is five, is now taking turns being the powerful one.

Tip: As you watch your three-year-old bully your innocent baby, try to remember that your children won't become frozen in wimp and bully roles. Sibling relationships and power struggles continually evolve. The child who is reigning chief this week may lose her power in a sibling coup next week.

Body Language Gives You Away   When Suzanne brought her third child home from the hospital, her two older sons were ages three and two. She tried to verbalize her understanding of their range of very mixed emotions. However, she soon realized that her body language belied what she was saying.

"I was saying to my two boys, 'It's okay to be angry,' but my neck and shoulders were stiffening every time I saw them even lightly tap the baby's foot. Sometimes it seemed as if my hand would instinctively reach out to push them away."

"My boys sensed that I was angry when they were the slightest bit aggressive toward the baby. Within three weeks, the older boy became subdued and the younger one was sucking his thumb and whining almost constantly. I also had a constant shoulder ache. My sister came over one day and really made me see what was going on. She said: 'You are just like Mom! You hover over the baby like she did every time I came within an inch of you. I used to feel so angry.' It then hit me that I was tense and scared when my boys showed any dislike toward the baby."

Tip: Lip service never works. Hard as we parents try to hide our feelings, our children almost always pick up on them. Parents have to really believe that it is acceptable for their toddler to have negative feelings toward siblings.

"I Can Do What You Can Do"   Nancy developed a nervous twitch when she was two and a half. At first her parents thought she was feeling overwhelmed in a new playgroup. But they soon discovered the real reason. One afternoon, Nancy was playing with her eighteen-month-old brother, who was just beginning to talk. Sure enough, every time he said a word, Nancy twitched. Her father decided that they should do a little downplaying. Rather than praise every new word with a round of applause, the parents simply described Daniel's achievement. "Oh, Daniel, I see you are really saying the word 'car.' " In less than a week, Nancy's twitch disappeared.

Tip: Whenever possible, try describing your child's action with enthusiasm rather than praising his efforts. This makes your toddler feel more confident and less bound to parental approval.

▼ ▼ ▼ ▼ ▼ ▼ ▼ ▼ ▼ ▼ ▼ ▼ ▼ ▼ ▼ ▼ ▼ ▼
Common Concerns

Q: My toddler seems to be constantly pushing, hitting, and basically making life miserable for my ten-month-old daughter. Should I never interfere?

You have to protect your baby from a toddler who treats her like a rag doll. But try not to make a big deal of your toddler's aggression. As soon as your baby is around one year old and more physically adept, she probably can handle a little more messing around from a toddler.

Q: Do you think that it is all right for a family to divide up on weekends? We have two children, and often my husband and I each take one child and spend time alone with that child.

As a steady diet and for long periods of time, dividing up may not be a great idea. If you are rarely together as a unit, you can be passing on the message that it is not fun to be together as a whole family. But I love the idea that at certain times each child gets special, individual attention from his parents.

Q: Is it a good idea to give presents to both my toddler and my other child when one of them has a birthday?

It's nice to give everyone who attends the party a favor. But the presents should go to the birthday child.

Q: When my three-year-old and my sixteen-month-old fight over toys, the older child always wins. This just doesn't seem fair.

When parents interfere, the fights almost always seem to escalate. In the very near future (it may even be happening now in small doses), your children will begin to negotiate. I know it is difficult advice to hear, but I recommend extending your threshold as much as you can.

Q: I like the idea of my children playing with each other's friends.

Your children should have the opportunity to develop their own friends. I don't think an older child should regularly baby-sit a younger sibling, nor should a younger child constantly tag along with an older sibling.

Summary

Sibling rivalry is a natural, normal situation because every child yearns to have his mother and father all to himself. When parents decide to play judge and intervene, the fights only become worse and the children angrier.

Your children will learn to resolve their own battles. They will also learn how to compete, negotiate, and love. Left to their own resources, each sibling will take turns playing the role of the helpless, misunderstood wimp and the hateful, mean-spirited bully. In truth, the less parents interfere, the less children will hurt each other and the less they remain locked into the role of "bully" or "wimp."

Sibling fights are training grounds for the real world. If you can trust your children to form their own relationships, the end result will be a loving, cherished one. Your children will also gain confidence and self-esteem.

However, staying out of your children's relationships does not mean that you ignore their feelings. Parents need to help their children articulate and understand their emotions. You don't want them growing up feeling bad about having "bad" feelings.

Remember, your children are allies. In every family the parents should stand firmly on one side and the children on the other.

▼ ▼ ▼ ▼ ▼ ▼ ▼ ▼ ▼ ▼ ▼ ▼ ▼ ▼ ▼ ▼ ▼ ▼

CHAPTER 12

Working Mothers

ANY PARENTS ASK ME IF I THINK IT IS TERRIBLE FOR A toddler to be separated from both parents all day. For the first few years, I would prefer one parent to be home at least part-time.

But is a toddler really harmed by a mother's absence? I believe that if a parent is basically satisfied with her life, whether staying at home or working full-time, the child will be well-adjusted. (One caveat: Replace yourself with someone who you trust and who really enjoys children.) Certainly a mother who feels frustrated as a full-time parent is going to have a more negative effect on a toddler than a contented mother who works. Says one lawyer with three children: "There is no doubt about it, the time I am the most frustrated is when I'm home after the birth of a child. So much of my ego is tied to my career." Admits another mother who works a three-day week: "I just can't sustain the level of interest for so many hours. By the end of the weekend I can't wait to get rid of my son. He's sick of me, too."

This chapter includes many suggestions from my parent groups about making life better for working mothers and toddlers. As almost every mother says, it isn't easy working, nor is it easy to be home with a toddler for twenty-four hours a day. Mothers who stay home mention feeling overwhelmed by caring for their children, whereas mothers who work often talk about never getting enough time with their children. While there is no perfect solution, it is crucial to find the work style that is best for you . . . and your toddler.

▼ ▼ ▼ ▼ ▼ ▼ ▼ ▼ ▼ ▼ ▼ ▼ ▼ ▼ ▼ ▼ ▼ ▼ ▼

How to Stay Sane and Work

1. Share with your partner. Don't always be the last to leave your home in the morning and the first to come home from work at night.

2. Ask for and accept as much help as you can get from relatives or any extended family you may adopt. If they want to shop or baby-sit say, "YES, YES, YES."

3. Work with your caregiver or daycare center to structure your toddler's day.

4. Call home and talk (even if it is just to say "I love you") to your toddler at least once a day. It is very reassuring for the both of you.

5. If your child is at a daycare center, whenever possible drop in for a short visit during the day.

6. Schedule important appointments, such as those with the pediatrician, for times you can be there.

7. Check out playground gossip about your caregiver or child. You want to be sure that life is going well when you are not around. For example, if a neighbor says that your baby-sitter is so busy talking to her friends that she barely interacts with your son, investigate before you either ignore the gossip or accuse your sitter.

8. Have a backup plan should the dreaded event occur—your baby-sitter gets sick. It would be ideal if you worked for a company with a drop-off emergency center or if you could leave your child at a trusted relative's house, but whatever your plan, be prepared.

9. Even if you feel you can't wait to tell your best friend some of the hottest gossip, it's better when you first come home to give your child some quality time. Leave your answering machine on or ignore the phone when you have that special time alone with your toddler.

10. Make a standing date with your partner. Hire a baby-sitter for one evening a week so that you have time alone together.

11. Have your partner take care of your toddler for a few hours on the weekend so that you have some time for yourself.

12. Don't let yourself get burned out. Instead of saving all your vacation time for the long, hot summer, take a long weekend in the fall, winter, and spring.

13. Save the caretaking tasks you enjoy, whether it's your toddler's bedtime story or bath, for yourself.

14. Don't blame the fact that you work as the cause of all your toddler's difficulties. At-home mothers have the same problems, for the most part, with their children.

15. Competition can drive you crazy. The fact is that many toddlers don't talk in sentences until they are three years old. The fact is that many toddlers don't know their colors until they are three. The fact is that many toddlers are bad sleepers. The fact is that many toddlers don't like giving up their diapers. The fact is that your child may not have a growth spurt until she is twenty-one years old!

▲ ▲ ▲ ▲ ▲ ▲ ▲ ▲ ▲ ▲ ▲ ▲ ▲ ▲ ▲ ▲ ▲ ▲ ▲

Your Past

Whether you need to work or choose to work, it's important to examine your own childhood. Often parents don't realize how much their past affects them until their children are born. Your own mother's working history is going to have a tremendous influence on your attitudes.

For instance, if you had a full-time working mother and felt that your needs were met, then you'll find it natural to work. However, if your mother resented working, felt guilty leaving you, and didn't provide the mothering you wanted, then you might have difficulty establishing a positive identity as a working mother. Says one mother: "My mother had to work for financial reasons and she really felt burdened. I now also have to work because I am the main breadwinner. I feel angry about being away so much from my child and I worry a lot."

Mothers also might have difficulty sorting out their own feelings if they see their jobs as a way to escape their mother's unhappy past and remain loyal to her memory. Says one mother with a three-year-old: "I had a full-time mother who would have been much happier and a better mom if she worked. I was exposed too much to her personality! She constantly was telling me how important it was to do something you enjoyed with your life. From the minute I was in college I was obsessed about having a career. When I had my children I was terrified about having my mom's frustration. Half the time I can't tell my real feelings about my job because I am so driven by this memory."

Once you understand how your past is influencing your feelings about work, it may affect your decision to work and your mothering. If you find yourself unable to resolve your issues about working, it may help to see a counselor.

How to Keep a Lid on Those Guilty Feelings

Parenting and guilt go hand in hand. It's almost a fact of life. So imagine all the guilt working mothers can feel! If you have to work late one week, you may feel guilty. If you spend half the evening on the phone with clients, you may feel guilty. If it seems that your toddler is the only one who brings his caregiver to playdates, you may feel guilty. If your toddler gets cold after cold (like every other two-year-old) but you still go to work, you may feel guilty. If your child sobs hysterically every morning when you leave for work, you may feel guilty.

First of all, it can be a relief just to acknowledge that you may always feel a little guilty working, because you aren't going to be the one taking care of your child's day-to-day needs. At times you may feel sad or jealous. "Oh no, I'm missing out on her first playground experience" (or "buying his sneakers," or "hearing her laugh"). At times the caregiver will do things that you wish you could do. At times your child may even seem to prefer your caregiver's company. You may sometimes feel a tremendous pull on your heartstrings and worry about your decision to work.

Once again, I basically believe that if parents take care of their needs and generally feel happy about working, that positivity will filter down to their children. When you leave for work in the morning, let your toddler see that you enjoy work. Instead of, "I wish I didn't have to work. I would much rather stay home with you," say, "I love you and will miss you. I'll be thinking of you." Don't make the farewell into a long-drawn-out affair.

Once at work, many mothers say the key to a better work and home life is to focus. You have your quality time at home with your toddler, now make work your focus time. When at work, be at work. However, if you find that you can't seem to stop worrying about your toddler, don't ignore your uneasiness. You may discover that you can't concentrate because your experience of being a parent is bringing up some of your own issues. Maybe you have difficulty saying good-bye and separating. Or there could be a legitimate reason for your anxiety. Says one mother: "I was constantly distracted by calling home and scheduling classes for my two-year-old. Sometimes these panic attacks would just come on me and I would worry that my daughter was hurt. I had this nagging feeling that my caregiver wasn't paying enough attention to her. Once I finally figured out that it just wasn't guilt, but real concern, I changed caregivers."

Going to work and having a child can call basic priorities into question. If you don't make conscious choices about your work style, your toddler probably will pick up on your ambivalence and feel as torn as you. Perhaps your partner will cut down on his hours because his schedule is more flexible. Perhaps you'll feel fine climbing up the ladder. Perhaps you will work part-time or change your job. Says one mother: "I felt so guilty because I was working very hard in this pressured ad agency. And even when I was home, even though I tried to be there for my son, I was always worrying about whether I would get my work done. I finally realized it was more important for me to have a less prestigious job and have a life outside. I now work full-time at an interesting job where the culture expects the day to end at six o'clock rather than midnight."

One suggestion that may sound simple: Try not to compare your choices with other mothers' choices. Many mothers say that they feel jealous and dissatisfied when they meet women who have decided to stay on the fast career path, just as many of these high rollers say that they feel selfish and guilty when they meet women on the mommy track. You need to make the choice that is right for you, not anyone else.

Time for Yourself

Does this sound familiar? "The only free time I get for myself is in the shower." "The only free time I get is the twenty minutes alone on the bus each day to work." "I would love to go to a gym but I feel really guilty leaving twenty minutes earlier each morning." "Friends, what friends! I just don't have time."

If parents don't get enough outlets for themselves, it can be hard to be relaxed or enthusiastic when they are with their toddler. Unfortunately, even mothers who manage to take some time for themselves often talk about how hard it is to tell their child they are going out for the sole purpose of enjoying themselves. They sneak out when their child is napping or they tell him they are going to work when they are really going to the movies. Tell your toddler the truth. Not only do you want her to trust you, but you also want her to learn that mothers and fathers need some time alone. "Mommy is going out with Daddy for dinner tonight. And you'll be staying with Gloria. After your bath Gloria will read you two special stories. When we come home we will come into your room and give you a big kiss." This type of explanation helps make your toddler feel secure because he knows that a specific plan has been set for him.

About That Quality Time

The concept of quality time can drive working parents crazy. Just because you work doesn't mean that you have to be on all the time when you are home. You can put your feet up and veg out. Your children are happy just to have you with them. Don't feel that you have to play and teach every second. By constantly being involved, parents can prevent their child from becoming a self-starter. The quality part of quality time means that when you do play with your child, you should really be there for her. If you feel distracted or bored, she'll pick up on your negative feelings.

I wish jobs required parents to take a few minutes for themselves and decompress before they went home to their children. While it might feel hard to delay your homecoming by ten minutes or so, the time spent unwinding gives you a chance to become a mother again. For example, one mother unwinds on her twenty-minute bus ride, one mother takes a brisk walk for ten minutes, and another picks up groceries and enjoys it. If you are able to unwind like this, when you do walk through the door you will have the energy to feel more connected to your toddler.

▼ ▼ ▼ ▼ ▼ ▼ ▼ ▼ ▼ ▼ ▼ ▼ ▼ ▼ ▼ ▼ ▼ ▼ ▼

Talk for Working Moms: How to . . .

1. Get your partner involved. Don't lay a guilt trip on him. Instead of, "You really are never here. I do everything. It's like being a single mom," try saying, "I really want you to have an impact on our child. You are very important to her and me. I know it's hard to believe that I'm not perfect, but I'd love her to have some of you in her."

2. Say good-bye. Keep it short and simple. You may think that parting is sweet sorrow, but your child just needs a few reassuring sentences from a decisive mother. "Honey, Mommy is going to work now. I'll call you at lunchtime. Tonight after dinner we'll read our special story. Bye-bye."

3. Plan your child's day with your caregiver. Don't apologize: "Do you mind if Kathy doesn't watch too much TV today?" "Do you mind bringing Kathy home from the park at three o'clock in time for a nap?" It works much better for you and your caregiver to be direct: "It's really important to us that Kathy doesn't watch more than one hour of television. We also worry that most programs are too old for her, so we would like her to watch only these tapes."

▲ ▲ ▲ ▲ ▲ ▲ ▲ ▲ ▲ ▲ ▲ ▲ ▲ ▲ ▲ ▲ ▲ ▲ ▲

How to Get Your Partner to Share Parenting Responsibilities

Many fathers who are no longer young parents say: "My biggest regret is that I did not spend enough time with my children when they were little. I see now that both my children and I missed out." It's doubly difficult if you and your partner work long work hours for both of you to be involved in parenting. Many mothers tell me how angry they feel because they expected their husband to share in the raising of their children but they find themselves doing at least 75 percent of the work. Says one mother who works as a teacher: "My husband passes three grocery stores on the way home. But does he ever buy milk? No. In fact it never seems to enter his mind. He just expects home life to run smoothly even though I work as much as he does."

What's so difficult about anger between parents is that not only does it make marriages miserable, but it also floats down to the children. Being the center of the universe, as all toddlers think they are, they may think that their bad thoughts and actions caused their parents to be angry. When resentments get very intense in families, a toddler can feel that she has to spend her day by her mother's side trying to get her to be a happy mommy again.

However, if you can manage to put aside your anger, which isn't always easy, some basic communication may nip your fury in the bud and rescue your toddler. Even though it might seem obvious to you that your partner should know he is not doing his fair share, he needs to hear it from you. Gather your thoughts and verbalize. Be reasonable and talk specifically about what you want him to do, for example, fix breakfast for the children because you aren't a morning person, or take your toddler to a Saturday playgroup, you may save yourself a lot of emotional wear and tear over the years. Setting up specific sessions to renegotiate who does what with your toddler can also help cut down on angry feelings. Some mothers consider who gets paid more and who works harder in order to decide whether they have the right to demand. But I've never known any parent who can successfully cut off anger long term by this type of reasoning.

One of the most crucial rules to follow if you really want your partner to share parenting is to let him have his own relationship with your toddler. While it can be hard for the parent who does most of the child care not to interfere, your partner should be able to do things his way. One mother explains: "I was really angry that my husband did not seem to be spending much time with our two-year-old. But on the other hand, when he finally was with our son I couldn't restrain myself from saying: 'Don't say that. It is not good for him. Do this.' I basically felt that I was the good and more knowledgeable parent because I spent more time with our child. My husband eventually exploded and said he didn't like spending time with me or our child when I was so critical."

What you expect from your partner as a partner and as a father is going to make a big difference in how he responds. Over the years I've noticed three styles in working mothers. There is the mother who essentially gives up on having her needs met and is constantly rationalizing: "What can I do? There is no way I can change him." Then there is the mother who is very confrontational but doesn't know how to get her needs met: "I'm so angry that you never do anything with our daughter. I am totally exhausted." The third kind of mother for the most part feels she is supported by her husband and accepts him for what he is. This couple have come to agree on certain rules. Consider this mother: "My husband and I have decided that the whole family is going to eat dinner together every night at eight o'clock. This is not always easy, since we work long hours at pressured jobs, but we rarely break the arrangement."

It is very important for partners to recognize the feelings they have toward each other, because bad feelings can pollute the atmosphere of an entire family. For example, if you find that when the whole family is finally together on weekends you and your partner aren't enjoying each other, figure out why. (Many parents say it helps to get as many chores done as possible on the weekdays. Any human being gets irritable when most of the day is spent running back and forth between the laundry and the grocery store with a toddler in tow.) Remember, everything between you and your partner may not be resolved by trying to talk on your own. Consider going to a couples counselor if it feels as though tensions aren't easing up.

If Your Toddler Is Having Trouble

It's been my observation that parents know when life is not going right with their toddler. Grandparents, aunts, friends, even teachers may tell you: "Oh don't worry. It's just a stage." But parents know in their gut when their toddler is not developing fully.

Don't assume that your working is the cause of your toddler's difficulties. Check out any worries you have about your toddler with your pediatrician. She might just be showing normal, age-appropriate behavior when she flings herself on the floor and screams because you said no. If you continue to be concerned about your toddler, seek the advice of a child therapist.

One mother tells this story: "I took the first year off from my job to stay with my son. I went back to work full-time after that. My son seemed in good hands with a woman I had known for many years because she worked at my aunt's house. I signed him up for gym classes and called other baby-sitters for playgroups. I also rushed to be home every night by six o'clock. Around the time he was twenty months old, I started to notice that he would cry hysterically in large groups and seemed very scared when people, even his grandparents, came to visit. At first I figured it was just a stage. Then, when he seemed to get more and more clingy at two and a half I began to get more worried. I also felt guilty because I was convinced that my not being home was having a bad effect on him. I decided to go to a therapist and to work part-time when he was three years old. The psychologist told me that my son's anxieties at this point had nothing to do with working. My son's problems weren't, as my mother kept suggesting, because of my work. He had developed fears that really needed professional help, which had nothing to do with me working part-time."

Paying for Lost Time

If you've been putting in a lot of late nights on the job, avoid making plans for nights out on the town. You don't want to over-schedule so that you are working, working, working and then socializing, socializing. Your toddler will suffer.

It's important to be aware that your actions do affect your child. When you work more than usual, try to schedule extra time with your child. You have to make up for lost hours, especially if your child is under stress because he's been sick or has a new baby-sitter. I know one mother who always takes off one day from work after she has a few long weeks or returns from a business trip. She says that this day not only gives her time to be with her children, but also gives the baby-sitter a needed break.

See if your partner can arrange to be home when you are working extra long hours. If your partner's schedule is similarly demanding, perhaps your parents or some other relatives can spend some special time with your children. One devoted grandmother cooks dinner and baby-sits when her lucky daughter works late.

Don't be surprised if your toddler makes you pay for your absence by being clingy, weepy, and angry. As she screams and refuses to look at you, try to remember that she wouldn't act out if she didn't love you and miss you so much.

It may seem excessive to offer an explanation to a two-year-old about your work schedule, but I recommend it. Toddlers are so egocentric that they may think you are working hard because they did something wrong. Say something like: "Mommy has to work a lot the next three days. But it's not your fault. Once my work is finished we are going to spend more time together. We'll go to the zoo on Thursday." Even if your toddler doesn't totally understand what you are saying, she'll catch enough of the gist to be reassured.

"Coffee break, Mommy!"

Summary

It's very hard to be satisfied, whether you work or stay home full-time. However, if you feel good about your job and you've been able to find a loving, trusted caregiver or daycare center, your toddler should fare well. What's important is that you find the work style that is best for you and your child.

It is crucial that you set up certain routines for both you and your child. For example, schedule the pediatrician's appointment for a time when you can be there. Work with your caregiver or daycare center to structure your toddler's day. Also, be sure to take care of yourself, even if it means taking an extra ten minutes to unwind before you come home.

If you are really ambivalent about whether to work or not, it could be that your own mother's life is influencing yours. Was she a homemaker who would rather have been in a chemistry lab than a kitchen? Was she a full-time worker who supported the family and never had any time for herself or for you?

Guilt and motherhood seem to go hand in hand. However, if you are a full-time working parent, you'll probably get a double dose of this feeling. Focus on work when you are at work, and check out any nagging worries about your child at home.

It is very hard, if you and your partner work long hours, to share parenting in a satisfactory way. However, it is crucial to negotiate a good working relationship with each other. Otherwise, your toddler will feel the resentments and suffer.

▼ ▼ ▼ ▼ ▼ ▼ ▼ ▼ ▼ ▼ ▼ ▼ ▼ ▼ ▼ ▼ ▼ ▼ ▼

CHAPTER 13

Caregivers

"ISPEND MORE TIME THINKING ABOUT MY CAREGIVER than about my husband!" say many mothers in my parent groups.

The caregiver relationship is one of the most complicated bonds parents will ever have. You want a perfect substitute for yourself, who will be nurturing and loving, but at the same time it can be hard to share your child. You want a caregiver who sincerely thinks that your child is the greatest in the world, despite the fact that you are paying for his or her services. You also may feel that your caregiver should always be there for your family, even though he or she is your caregiver and not your mother.

In my caregiver workshops I've seen over and over how, even with the best intentions, the relationship can become confused. As parents handing over our most precious asset, it can be hard to accept that we are hiring a professional. Families who are very happy with their caregiver usually aren't just lucky; they know the type of person they want and how to communicate.

What Type of Person Do You Want?

Before you even begin interviewing caregivers, it's essential to look at yourself. You are bringing another person into your family and you have to be honest about the type of person you feel comfortable with. While your caregiver doesn't have to be your best friend, you have to be able to work with him or her.

Of course, every parent wants someone who is warm, smart, kind, patient, responsible, and honest. But try going beyond these basic traits.

Do you want a perky young person who likes to be involved in your life or an older person who keeps a distance? Do you want someone who is outgoing or quiet? Do you want someone who can take control and plan the day? Or do you prefer a caregiver who will be more comfortable if the parent takes the lead? Do you care if your caregiver is organized and neat? Do you want your caregiver to have a similiar style to you and your partner in setting limits?

Consider the differences in the preferences of two mothers.

"Good answer! Ok–question number 349: How do your views on world peace affect your thoughts on childcare?"

Says a full-time mother of three children: "I want a young live-in caregiver. Someone who is like me, casual, outgoing, upbeat. I could never deal with an older woman who wanted to boss me and my children around. I want someone who is comfortable eating with our family at meals and doesn't need specific tasks or hours. I want someone who can do her own thing. I'm not bothered by a caregiver who comes in at 2 A.M. after a night out on the town if she is responsible." The other mother, who works a five-day week in an office, wants stricter limits with a caregiver: "I like it when I can maintain my privacy. I also would prefer an older woman who is very organized and able to adjust to our plans. As long as she is good with my children, I don't think I need to get involved with the details of her life."

Job Description

Once parents have figured out the type of person they're looking for, the next step is defining the job. Every possible detail, not only hours, but vacations, overtime pay, and so on, should be spelled out. In my caregiver workshops I've watched relationships quickly sour when parents didn't set forth clear expectations.

The nature of the job may change over time, but it is important for your caregiver to know exactly what he or she is getting into. Don't take anything for granted. Start the relationship on the right foot by being direct.

If you want your caregiver to clean, shop, or cook dinner, say so, and be specific. For example, by cleaning do you mean just taking care of the children's rooms and clothes? (Keep in mind that taking good care of a toddler is an extremely demanding job, so don't swamp the caregiver with too many other responsibilities.) You might try setting up a list of priorities for your caregiver. One mother voices her regrets: "I was so anxious about finding a caring person who would fall absolutely in love with my two-year-old that I didn't want to even discuss the 'less important' parts of the job. That was a big mistake. My caregiver really resents that I now want her to cook dinner and do laundry. In fact, I feel so intimidated that I still don't even ask her to do simple shopping."

It pays to go overboard in listing the negatives of the job. If you and your partner are sometimes late coming home from work, say so. If your very opinionated mother-in-law comes over daily, tell the applicant. If you want the caregiver to sleep over one night a week, break the news now.

I would also recommend talking about how the job may change. Confess if you are planning to have another child within the year. If you know you are going to send your toddler to nursery school in one year, tell the caregiver that he or she will be responsible for more housework. Says one mother: "My caregiver quit after one year. She said she thought she had been hired just to take care of my two daughters. She didn't want to clean even after both daughters were in nursery school."

How to Find a Caregiver

Agencies, ads in local newspapers, and other parents can provide you with names. (In fact, more names than you probably want.) You also might get some good leads from your pediatrician, a local preschool and daycare center bulletin board, or by asking caregivers you like.

Even if you think you have found the caregiver of your dreams on the first interview, I'd recommend still seeing a handful of people. The more people you talk to, the more perspective you will gain. But there is a point at which too many interviews can become confusing. Recalls one mother: "My husband and I interviewed thirty people. I kept thinking there must be the perfect person somewhere out there. But I got so burned out, I couldn't tell who I liked. I ended up hiring someone who had worked for a friend of a friend. This caregiver has turned out to be really good for us."

It is easy to feel overwhelmed. Many parents tell me that an ad in a local paper can bring in dozens of calls. In this case an answering machine can help with initial screening if applicants are asked to leave their years of experience and references. Says one father: "Of the dozens of responses I got from my ad, I called back only four people. I crossed off many names right away because they didn't have experience or because they ignored my questions on the answering machine. Some people also just sounded out of it."

Of course, it can be reassuring to hire the caregiver that your best friend used. But even this close connection doesn't guarantee that your family's needs will be met. People have different expectations and likes. Says one father: "We hired the caregiver of a prominent pediatrician. We felt that if this person was good enough for her, she would be perfect for us. Guess what? Not only did we find the caregiver's personality grating, but we really didn't trust her. She seemed forgetful and lazy."

Keep in mind when you call past references that many people give unjustified rave reviews. Why? Perhaps they feel guilty because they fired the person, or perhaps they think he or she was good enough. You have to be very specific with a former employer to get a true perspective. Try asking how often the caregiver was late or sick, what his or her favorite activity with the children was, whether the caregiver made playdates, whether he or she was flexible about staying in the evenings, if the caregiver came to work cranky or was bothered when a child wouldn't listen, and if the parents found it easy to talk to the caregiver about their children.

Don't rush to make a decision. If you lose a caregiver because you didn't hire him or her on the spot, so be it. There is another person out there for your family. You want to give yourself ample time to feel comfortable and satisfied.

▼ ▼ ▼ ▼ ▼ ▼ ▼ ▼ ▼ ▼ ▼ ▼ ▼ ▼ ▼ ▼ ▼ ▼

Sample Advertisement

Looking for a warm, loving, honest caregiver to live out/in. Must have experience working with toddlers. English a prerequisite. Recent references with phone numbers. Nonsmoker.

▲ ▲ ▲ ▲ ▲ ▲ ▲ ▲ ▲ ▲ ▲ ▲ ▲ ▲ ▲ ▲ ▲ ▲

▼ ▼ ▼ ▼ ▼ ▼ ▼ ▼ ▼ ▼ ▼ ▼ ▼ ▼ ▼ ▼ ▼ ▼ ▼

The Interview

In the best of all worlds both parents should be at the interviews. At the very least, both parents should meet a caregiver before any final decision is made. You and your partner very well may have different reactions to the caregivers. You also want to let the caregivers see right from the start that both parents are involved in child care.

I'd recommend having your toddler around for at least part of the interview. While almost every caregiver will claim to love children, you might pick up some sense of the caregiver's style if your toddler tries to empty her pocketbook or runs around his chair twenty times. The bottom line is that you want someone who is patient and enjoys children, particularly toddlers. A good caregiver should also be able to follow your toddler's lead and not overwhelm your child with his or her own personality.

You may want to use the following interview questions to gain some insight into your applicants.

1. What do you enjoy about child care?

2. What do you find most difficult?

3. What do you want out of the job?

4. Do you have any preference in terms of a child's sex or age? (You probably are not going to hire someone who prefers helpless, cuddly babies.)

5. How do you set limits?

6. How do you deal with toilet training?

7. What don't you like to do as a caregiver?

8. How do you like to spend a typical day with a toddler?

9. Does a toddler's mess drive you crazy?

10. How do you feel about toddlers' being difficult so often?

11. Why did you leave your last job? (The family moved, the nature of the job changed, and the caregiver no longer wanted to live in are all legitimate reasons for moving on.)

12. What are your career plans?

13. How much involvement do you want and expect with the parents?

Words of advice: Follow your gut reaction; chemistry does count. The most articulate caregiver may not necessarily be the best. And, if you have to convince yourself, don't hire.

▲ ▲ ▲ ▲ ▲ ▲ ▲ ▲ ▲ ▲ ▲ ▲ ▲ ▲ ▲ ▲ ▲ ▲ ▲ ▲

Trial Runs

Many parents find it helpful to call back a few caregivers they liked in the interviews, pay them for a day's work, and take a closer look. Test runs can be tiresome because they entail spending the day talking to the caregiver and watching his or her every move with your toddler. But remember that you will be entrusting your pride and joy to someone else's care. Feelings of basic trust, comfort, and give-and-take are crucial.

When you spend eight hours with a caregiver, you will probably see traits you didn't notice in the interview. Says one mother: "We would have hired this woman if I hadn't spent a day with her. She spent most of the time talking about her boyfriend. And when I served her lunch she didn't even bother bringing her plates to the sink. I also didn't like how she interacted with my daughter. She didn't pick up at all on my daughter's personality. She was constantly tickling her, rolling on the floor with her, and taking over."

For another mother, who went through a battery of baby-sitters after her longtime caregiver left, day two of a trial run made her see that one caregiver wasn't right for her. Says this mother: "I was just about to hire this caregiver but decided I would give her one more trial day. It was a good thing I did! Her friends obviously thought I had gone out. She got about ten phone calls during the day!"

Establishing Good Communications

It's essential to make communication a number one priority. Your caregiver is in a service business (your family is the client), and issues will come up that need airing. If your caregiver feels that it is difficult to talk with you, he or she may resent you or misunderstandings may arise. Also, remember that you are teaching your toddler the meaning of *respect* when you show her that you value the caregiver's opinions and feelings.

So, how do you get your caregiver to feel comfortable enough to communicate? I've noticed that when people use themselves as an example it often helps to open up another person. For instance I might say something like, "It really drives me crazy when Liz is so clingy. For the last two weeks she's seemed to be glued to me. I can imagine how you feel when it seems as though she is choosing me over you."

Try to build in a few minutes every day for some overlap time—as you are drinking coffee or straightening up the kitchen—to have informal, ongoing chats. Find out what your child did during the day, what type of mood he was in, how long he napped. Talk *before* problems build up. Remember, your caregiver is a person with a life outside work. Take an interest in your caregiver's personal life. Ask about his or her family. Says one mother: "My caregiver always seemed in such a grumpy mood when she walked in the door every morning. I think she felt I barely noticed her before I ran out the door for work. Now that we talk every day she seems to be much happier. I think she appreciates that I treat her as an important person in my family's life."

Who is responsible for planning your child's day? Parents often complain that they have to do everything. However, it may not be that your caregiver lacks initiative, but that he or she thinks that you want to plan the activities. If you would prefer your caregiver to make playdates, say so.

I would also recommend a formal discussion at least once a month. This should be a designated time when parents can talk about their concerns and share their philosophy on such issues as setting limits and eating. Be as specific as possible if you want your caregiver to follow your philosophy. Says one father: "I told my caregiver that if my two-and-a-half-year-old doesn't listen, she can give her time-out for three minutes. I said under no condition did I ever want her to hit her."

Also be sure to ask your caregiver if anything is bothering him or her about the job or your child. Says one mother: "I thought my caregiver was very happy in her job until we asked her. She said that it was too much work to clean now that she had to take care of the new baby as well as the toddler. She also said she felt that the three-year-old was old enough to pick up his own toys." In this instance, the parents realized that the caregiver was right, took over basic cleaning, and began to insist that their son do his own picking up.

It is important to have these meetings at a time that is convenient for both parents and caregiver. The talks should not take place in the presence of your toddler or, if possible, after your caregiver's official hours. Understandably, your caregiver may be resentful if you begin an earnest talk right when he or she is supposed to go home.

Just as you expect to be rewarded at a job, so you should acknowledge your caregiver's good work with annual raises (even if you can only afford small increases). If you are not satisfied enough to give a raise, then the caregiver shouldn't be working at your home.

Bonuses also can be wonderful ways to show special appreciation. I know one family that gave their caregiver two extra weeks of pay for having been so helpful with their ill newborn.

▼ ▼ ▼ ▼ ▼ ▼ ▼ ▼ ▼ ▼ ▼ ▼ ▼ ▼ ▼ ▼ ▼ ▼ ▼

Making Your Caregiver Feel That He or She Counts

1. Have your caregiver's wages ready on payday.

2. Come home when expected.

3. Give enough advance notice about your vacations for your caregiver to plan time off as well.

4. Don't let your child put the caregiver in a humiliating situation. For example, don't let your toddler have food fights with his older sister and then expect the caregiver to clean up.

5. Be sure that both you and your partner greet your caregiver each morning.

6. If you work at home, don't interfere constantly.

7. Let your toddler know that he must listen to the caregiver's no's.

8. Let the caregiver know in advance when you make playdates.

9. Ask whether your caregiver minds having playdates with parents rather than with other caregivers.

10. Leave emergency and daily money.

11. Have food for your caregiver to eat.

12. Ask your caregiver about his or her own family.

▲ ▲ ▲ ▲ ▲ ▲ ▲ ▲ ▲ ▲ ▲ ▲ ▲ ▲ ▲ ▲ ▲ ▲

Just a Little Bit of Respect

If your caregiver doesn't feel respected, he or she is not going to feel good about the job. And unless your caregiver is a saint, these negative thoughts will float down to your child. Thank your caregiver for doing a good job and be considerate of your caregiver's feelings and time. Like everyone else who works, your caregiver wants to know that his or her efforts are noticed and that you have faith in him or her.

Parents sometimes lose sight of the fact that their caregiver is not merely an employee. If you trust your caregiver with your child, don't ask for receipts for everything he or she buys for your house. Or, if you come home early and want some time alone with your toddler, don't make your caregiver stay on until the end of the official workday, as if using a time card.

Although many mothers say that they are much more involved in the caregiver relationship than are their husbands, caregivers expect to be treated with respect by both parents. One caregiver felt incredibly hurt by the following incident: "I twisted my ankle on my way to work. It hurt terribly all day. At five o'clock the husband walked in and saw me with my leg up on a chair. He barely said hello. I could tell he was angry. The next day the wife asked me why I seemed to be sleeping on the job. I felt very bad that the father couldn't confront me himself. I thought we had a good relationship."

Structure Your Toddler's Day

Says one mother: "With my first child I felt almost apologetic when I asked my caregiver to do certain things with her. I started every request with 'Do you mind?' So when I was at work I was constantly worrying about what they were doing. I had this horrible image of my daughter sitting depressed in front of the television." Just because a mother spends the day at work doesn't mean that she has to relinquish responsibility for her child. You want to feel comfortable about your toddler's care when you are away. If you have definite ideas about what you want your child to eat, when the caregiver should say no, or how long your child's playdates should be, say so.

However, as important as it is to shape your toddler's day, you won't get the best from your caregiver if you merely hand over daily lists of activities and meals. Try to involve your caregiver in the planning. A caregiver who feels trusted and appreciated and is allowed to use his or her own judgement will be better with your child. Ask daily how life is going: "So, how was your day today with Ellen? I found her in a bad mood when she woke up. Did things improve? How'd you handle it when she wanted to stay in the park longer?" One mother I know finds it helpful to leave a diary so that her caregiver can write what time her daughter naps, eats, and so on. "This way I don't feel like I'm cross-examining her," she says.

When parents don't communicate regularly and respectfully with their caregiver, the child almost always seems to lose out. Only a caregiver with the character of a saint can keep feelings about the child's parents from affecting the relationship with the child. Says one mother: "I was sending my toddler twice a week to this very formal playgroup with my caregiver. I just expected her to go and I never asked her whether she or my son enjoyed it. About six months into the group she suddenly said: 'Oh, Richard hates it so much. He cries and doesn't move out of my lap.' I then went to the group and realized it wasn't right for my son. I felt so bad that I had forced this whole experience on both of them. From now on I constantly ask my caregiver for her take on Richard's day. She isn't the type of person to initiate these conversations, but I think now that we talk she is less intimidated."

Of course, you have to trust your caregiver and the kind of person he or she is. You also have to remember that every parent has a different style and comfort level with his or her caregiver. One mother, who has had the same caregiver for ten years, rarely tells her what to do with her toddler. "I check in with her at least once a day but I totally trust her. She makes almost all my child's playdates. I work 'til 7:30 every evening. When I'm home I want to be with my two-year-old, not on the phone planning his next playdate."

Another mother, who had a disastrous situation with a caregiver because she let her make almost all the decisions, now takes the opposite approach. "I hired a caregiver the second time around who really wanted me to take charge. My last caregiver didn't want plans from me nor did she want to make plans herself. (She seemed to spend the day in the house reading magazines.) I feel much more comfortable at my job when I pretty much know what my toddler is doing every hour."

Some mothers, particularly those with type A personalities, purposely hire low-key, calm caregivers. "My baby-sitter is the type of person who will stop to show my toddler the leaves. Me, I am more apt to teach my daughter the ABCs than new leaves," says one mother.

But even if you do employ a patient, tireless person, don't expect your caregiver to be in the entertainment business. After all, could you keep your child stimulated for ten hours a day, or, for that matter, would you really want someone to occupy him so totally? Every toddler needs some time alone to learn how to entertain himself, just as your caregiver needs some down time.

How to Tell Your Toddler When a Caregiver Leaves

However important a child's relationship with her caregiver, re-member that it is the parents who will remain constant in their child's life. Caregivers will come and go. Although it is difficult for your toddler to say good-bye, she will adjust.

If you know that your caregiver is leaving, tell your child a few days in advance. For instance, if your caregiver is going to computer programming school, say something like: "Jenny is leaving to go to school. She will always love you. And it is not your fault that she is leaving. Let's think of a special way to say good-bye."

You may want to help your toddler pick out a present and even have a small party with a cake. Take a photo of the caregiver with your family. Give one picture to your caregiver and one to your toddler.

However, if you had to fire your caregiver on the spot for some horrible act, like leaving your toddler alone in the house, you will not be able to prepare your child. You might say something like:

"Jenny was not the right person to take care of you. We will find someone who is. It is not your fault she is leaving. Mommy and Daddy will always be here for you."

It is key when a caregiver leaves for your toddler to feel in no way responsible. Whether your caregiver chooses to leave or is fired, it is very important to say: "It is not your fault Jenny is leaving. You didn't do anything to make Jenny leave." Remember at this age your child thinks he's the cause of everything good and bad that happens in the universe.

Firing: When It's Time to Change Caregivers

Sometimes parents will keep a caregiver they aren't comfortable with just because they know that he or she is reliable or they think that they couldn't do better. I have often heard parents say with great resignation, "She isn't great, but how do I know I could find anyone better?"

Other times the fear and guilt of firing someone make parents discount their feelings. "I don't really like her, but she is great with my child."

The bottom line is that parents should feel good about their caregiver. If you have any hesitation or awkward feelings about the caregiver, he or she is not right for your child. Says one mother: "It was such an emotional thing for me to fire my caregiver. I felt so guilty that I gave her two months of extra pay. There was nothing really wrong with her but I always had an uneasy feeling when I left my daughter with her. I felt that she just wasn't paying enough attention to her. Now that we have a new person I know what it means to feel good about a caregiver. My child has come out of her shell and seems so much more spontaneous."

If your caregiver's lifestyle or past history with her own family seems to be overwhelming her on the job, it may also be wise to look elsewhere. Says one father: "I had to fire our caregiver because she was always favoring the younger child. It turned out that in her family her older brother was very mean to her."

Another parent found that the caregiver didn't work out because of exactly what she had hired her for: experience. Says this mother: "At first I thought it was great that she had been the oldest of eleven children. She seemed so knowledgeable. However, I began to realize that, although she was experienced, she resented being stuck taking care of children again."

▼ ▼ ▼ ▼ ▼ ▼ ▼ ▼ ▼ ▼ ▼ ▼ ▼ ▼ ▼ ▼ ▼ ▼ ▼

From the Caregiver's Point of View

Yes, they do compare wages and hours. So don't think you can underpay and overwork and still have your caregiver feel good about the job.

An issue that often emerges in my caregiver workshop is how hard it is to be honest. Many caregivers feel that they might lose their job if they report something unpleasant or unsuccessful, such as their charge hitting another child on a playdate or falling off a slide. (Parents, remember, you need to make your caregiver feel comfortable enough to be open.) Below are some common thoughts:

1. "I'm afraid I'll be fired if I say I need a break in the day. I'd like to take a rest when Tom naps but I'm afraid to ask."

2. "It just is too much work for me to clean and take care of the baby and toddler."

3. "Maybe once a month my train is late. I always call from the station but I still feel the parents don't believe me when I say the train was late."

4. "I never know where I stand. The parents never compliment me. They always seem to be in a rush or tired. I feel sort of taken for granted."

5. "I can't believe they don't check in during the day. I never even know what time they are coming home from work."

6. "The parents are giving me the feeling that I'm not doing my job correctly because Tim cries when they leave and come home. But when Tim is with me he's fine; he laughs, eats, naps, and seems happy."

7. "I feel angry when the mom checks up on me to make sure I haven't given Barbara anything sweet. I feel like she is just looking to find something wrong because she doesn't trust me."

▲ ▲ ▲ ▲ ▲ ▲ ▲ ▲ ▲ ▲ ▲ ▲ ▲ ▲ ▲ ▲ ▲ ▲ ▲

▼ ▼ ▼ ▼ ▼ ▼ ▼ ▼ ▼ ▼ ▼ ▼ ▼ ▼ ▼ ▼ ▼ ▼ ▼

Common Concerns

Q: My caregiver's moodiness is driving me crazy. She seems cheerful with my children, but is often quite cranky with me.

First of all, children definitely feel the tension when the parents don't have a pleasant, solid relationship with the caregiver. Try to straighten out the problem by directly asking your caregiver why she seems so moody. Is there something bothering her on the job or at home? If your caregiver can't rise above her moodiness, she isn't for you. You want an even-tempered professional taking care of your children.

Q: I'm embarrassed to admit this, but I am jealous of my caregiver's relationship with my two-year-old.

It is hard to share your child with another person. However, if you really think about how wonderful it is that your toddler has such a good relationship, perhaps your jealousy will fade.

But if the relationship continues to make you jealous, it's important to think about why you are so bothered. In your heart of hearts do you feel guilty that you aren't spending enough time with your child? I also would recommend talking to your caregiver about your feelings. You don't want your caregiver to think she should have a distant relationship with your toddler just to cool your jealousy.

Q: My caregiver has a daughter who is exactly the same age as my two-and-half-year-old daughter. I worry that this complicates her relationship with my child.

This really depends on the caregiver. If she sees herself as a professional on the job and can separate her personal life, this situation should be fine. If, however, she seems to be constantly comparing the children, then the situation is not good.

You also have to consider whether she is burned out from taking care of two toddlers—one at her house and one at yours.

Q: My caregiver was great with my son as a baby but doesn't seem as good now that he is a toddler.

Anyone who takes care of your child will have to learn how to respond to his growth. I believe it is the parents' responsibility to discuss changes in their child with the caregiver. If you feel good about your caregiver and your caregiver loves your toddler, most likely he or she will learn how to adapt to each year.

That said, there are certain people who have enormous preferences for certain ages. No matter how frequent the discussions with parents, some caregivers just don't enjoy an older child as much, particularly a difficult toddler. If this is the case, you need to look for a new caregiver.

Q: The minute I walk in the door from work my caregiver rushes out to go home. This really bothers me.

Consider, do you rush out to work the minute your caregiver arrives at your house in the morning? That can make your caregiver feel taken for granted.

Also, you can't expect your caregiver to sit and chat if you come home at 5:30, exactly when he or she is supposed to go home. Talk with your caregiver about wanting some time together at the end of the day. You will either have to come home ten minutes earlier or extend her hours with pay.

Q: My caregiver spends much of the day with other friends who are caregivers. Is this bad for my toddler?

As long as your caregiver is giving your child the attention he needs, I think it is fine for your caregiver to see other caregiver friends. You want your child socialized. Just as you probably need a group of friends who are warm and supportive on the job or at home, so does your caregiver.

Q: I feel as though I am constantly telling my caregiver how to act in every situation with my toddler. Am I undermining her authority?

It just doesn't work to act like a sergeant commanding an inexperienced recruit. You want to show some respect for your caregiver's own experience and background.

However, you do want to get your basic views across. You probably want to make sure that your child has a regular schedule, eats healthy foods, and is not scared into good behavior. One mother told me that her caregiver got her toddler to stop crying through scare tactics such as these: "The car is going to be very angry at you and drop you off if you don't stop crying."

You also probably want to hear how your caregiver would act in certain situations. For example, how would she react if the older brother were picking on the younger brother? What would she say if your child hit another child?

The big thing about talking together is for your caregiver to hear what bothers you, and vice versa. Remember, if you don't like something, you have to tell your caregiver. But once you've spoken your mind, don't drive your caregiver crazy about every little thing.

Q: I'm worried that my daughter is not happy with my caregiver. Every morning when I leave for work she starts sobbing. It breaks my heart.

This sobbing could really have nothing to do with your daughter's feelings for her caregiver. She could just be having a hard time separating from you. That's to be expected from a toddler.

If you listen outside the door I bet that your daughter will stop crying in about one minute. However, if your caregiver tells you that he or she is unable to console your daughter, I would take a hard look at the caregiver. I also would think about whether the caregiver is right for your daughter, if you notice that day after day she seems very subdued or unresponsive when you return home.

Q: My caregiver works five days a week from 8:30 to 5:00. I need to be out two nights a week. Before I hire someone else, should I ask her if she wants to work these evenings? (I've hesitated because it seems such a long day for her.)

I would definitely discuss the situation with her. You don't want to insult your caregiver. Make certain that you tell her that her response will in no way affect her job. If she would like to try working the extra hours, fine.

Q: What should I say to my caregiver about punishing my toddler?

This is one area of child rearing I'd be very clear about. While I would not allow anyone to hit my child, it is important for the caregiver to have the power to set limits. A firm "No, you may not do that" is often very effective. If your toddler seriously misbehaves, you might allow your caregiver to give a two-minute time-out.

You have to empower your caregiver to stop a situation that he or she can't tolerate, such as throwing food on the floor. But also make sure your caregiver understands that you don't expect your child to be a saint.

Q: My caregiver lives in and I wonder if I should be allowing my toddler to sleep in her bed?

Through my parent groups I hear that this is a fairly common habit. The problems that can arise are almost the same as those that can arise if your child is sleeping in your bed. (Of course, the difference is that you get to sleep.)

You want your child to experience being alone. You also don't want to burden the caregiver with exhausting nights of little sleep. I would try to stop this habit right away. Both you and the caregiver should tell your child that she can no longer sleep in the caregiver's bed and that you, the parent, will help her learn how to get to sleep alone.

Q: I came home unexpectedly and found my son looking dejected in front of the television.

This situation would make most parents feel sad, guilty, and angry. However, before assuming that your son has been staring sadly at a television for hours I would talk with the caregiver.

You have to find out if your son just came home from a playdate exhausted, or if this type of mood and activity is a steady diet. If it turns out that he is watching too much television, sit down and tell your caregiver how much television you want your son to watch. You might also suggest activities they can do together, such as cooking.

Summary

Choosing a caregiver in many ways is like choosing a partner. Your relationship with your caregiver can influence your happiness, your toddler's well-being, and your total family's functioning. Families who are very happy with their caregiver know themselves well enough to understand the type of person they want. Do you prefer someone young and energetic? Or do you prefer someone more maternal and take-charge?

Local newspapers, agencies, and word-of-mouth will provide some good leads. Although it is essential to call references, you must ask very detailed questions to get a total picture of the person. It is also very important to have some well-thought-out questions when you interview a caregiver—for example, you might ask what the applicant wants to get out of the job, how limits are set, whether he or she is bothered by a toddler's "No's." Giving trial runs will also help parents learn about the caregiver's style. As in your own experience, your caregiver's past history greatly affects how he or she addresses your toddler's needs. For instance, if she was the oldest child from a large family, how did she feel about taking care of all her brothers and sisters?

Communication with your caregiver should be a number one priority. It doesn't have to be long, but it should be every day. How was your child's mood during a playdate? How long did he nap? What did she eat for snack? And of course, how was the day for your caregiver? Be sure to make your caregiver feel that he or she counts. It goes almost without saying that the person who takes care of your toddler should be treated as sensitively as you want your child treated.

▼ ▼ ▼ ▼ ▼ ▼ ▼ ▼ ▼ ▼ ▼ ▼ ▼ ▼ ▼ ▼ ▼

CHAPTER 14

Family Vacations

ALTHOUGH EVERY MOMENT OF OUR MANY FAMILY VA-cations wasn't perfect, the experiences remain some of the most memorable in our lives. When my husband and I took our three children away to new places, we saw the surroundings through their young eyes. And even though the trips were often a nightmare to organize, we returned home renewed as a family.

We still laugh over the night my husband sat at a different table in a restaurant pretending not to know us. We reminisce about the infamous ferry crossing from Bar Harbor, Maine to Nova Scotia, Canada. My two-year-old daughter and three-year-old son and I lay prostrate on the floor, seasick, throwing up breakfast, as my husband and six-year-old son ministered to us.

So is this often-exhausting experience worth it all? Definitely yes. But first take a deep breath, and remember to pack realistic expectations along with the clothes.

▼ ▼ ▼ ▼ ▼ ▼ ▼ ▼ ▼ ▼ ▼ ▼ ▼ ▼ ▼ ▼ ▼ ▼ ▼

Expectations

1. Don't expect this to be a vacation on which you and your partner will experience your most tender and intimate moments.

2. Expect your toddler to act his usual charming self. No matter what elegant hotel you may stay at, he is still going to show you his worst and best sides. In fact, he may impress you with especially outrageous behavior until he gets used to his surroundings and routine.

3. Don't expect to spend your days doing what you want to do.

4. Expect to have periods when you wonder why you ever decided to attempt such togetherness.

5. Don't expect to transform your child's personality in two weeks.

6. Expect to return home more in touch with your family but at least as tired as when you left.

▲ ▲ ▲ ▲ ▲ ▲ ▲ ▲ ▲ ▲ ▲ ▲ ▲ ▲ ▲ ▲ ▲ ▲ ▲

How Parents' Attitudes Can Make or Break a Vacation

Read how two fathers interact with their toddlers on day one of a trip. Who do you think will have the better vacation?

Dad One: "No, we can't go to the bathroom again! Just sit still and look out the airplane window. I think I brought you a toy but I just have to find it. Don't throw anything on the floor. You are hungry again? You'll just have to wait like everyone else for lunch."

Dad Two: "Boy, it's fun going to the bathroom on the plane. It's like a roller coaster. Now let me take out your special surprise bag. We'll just put everything on the tray and pick up later. My stomach

Father: "Whose kids are these?"
Mother: "Yours, Bob."

is grumbling with all this flying. Help me spread our picnic. Mom and I packed it last night when you were sleeping."

Where to Go

We've all heard tales of parents who take their toddler on a whirlwind tour of the great museums of Europe. What we usually don't hear is that these parents often end up touring the great playgrounds of the Western world.

Most parents do compromise on the type of vacation they take if they are traveling with toddlers. Your best bet is to pick a spot that has plenty of child-friendly activities available, whether it is a beach resort, a ranch, or a motel with a soda machine and a pool.

The vacation doesn't have to be fancy or expensive. It can simply be a week camping out by a lake or staying at Grandma's house. Swimming, parks, zoos, and other children (not gourmet dining and sightseeing) make a vacation for a two-year-old. Call the local chamber of commerce; such activities are bound to be no more than an hour away from most locations. Also, seek out a place with calm water or a kiddie pool. You probably don't want your toddler riding the surf.

If you do plan to stay in a hotel, don't even think about booking a room if the brochure says that children over age twelve are welcome. And if you are staying in a hotel for more than a long weekend, seriously contemplate whether you will find it bearable to live together in one room. Or, even if you can reserve two connecting rooms, think about whether you will climb the walls without a kitchen. Just imagine three meals a day in a restaurant with your toddler! If there is a choice between elegant dining or a snack bar, go for the hamburger and grilled cheese meal plan at kiddie prices and hours. Consider one mother's plight: "We spent ten days in an expensive hotel. But my stomach still churns thinking of eating three meals a day in restaurants with my twenty-eight-month-old daughter screaming and jumping in her high chair. The only good result: I lost seven pounds."

Condominium resorts or cottage colonies definitely have advantages. People go to these facilities expecting kids, noise, and kitchens. You also may want to look at resorts that bill themselves as loving families. If you choose not to leave your toddler in the playgroups there, you won't have to look very far to find other activities. Renting a house that includes use of nearby resort facilities can be a good compromise for families who want more privacy. Says one mother: "We rent a house in Florida right next to the two beach resorts. This way our toddler can scream at 6 A.M. and run around the dining room table fifty times at dinner without disturbing anyone but his poor parents. The disadvantages: housework and shopping."

Every family has its own priorities and tolerance level. One family with a thirty-month-old boy took the opposite approach to a vacation by steering away from other children. They signed on to a tour for senior citizens! Says the father: "It was perfect. The trip was a very leisurely bus tour out West with just a few planned activities a day. Most of the people were grandparents, and they fell in love with our toddler."

You might find it difficult to find a senior citizen tour so enthusiastic about a two-year-old traveling companion. Most toddlers and parents also find it more relaxing to stay in one location.

Sleeping in a new bed every night can be trying. But be creative, and read up. Several books and travel agents now focus on family vacations and resorts for all kinds of budgets.

▼ ▼ ▼ ▼ ▼ ▼ ▼ ▼ ▼ ▼ ▼ ▼ ▼ ▼ ▼ ▼ ▼ ▼ ▼ ▼

Preparations

1. Get the name of a local doctor from your pediatrician.

2. Bring along emergency medicine suggested by your pediatrician.

3. Pack your child's most precious toys, books, and bedding.

4. Try to get the hotel to supply as much as possible: crib, high chair, even stroller.

5. Don't scrimp on the amount of clothing you bring for your toddler unless you want to spend most of the day in the laundry room.

▲ ▲ ▲ ▲ ▲ ▲ ▲ ▲ ▲ ▲ ▲ ▲ ▲ ▲ ▲ ▲ ▲ ▲ ▲ ▲

Drop-in Programs

If you vacation at a resort with a children's program, it is tempting to think you've found paradise on earth. After all, you can have some time alone as your toddler happily amuses herself with other children, ice cream parties, and sandbox wars.

But before you sign your toddler up for the week, there are some considerations. First of all, not only is your child sleeping in a strange bed in a new environment, but he is now expected to spend part of his day coping without his mother or father. This could be a difficult separation, particularly if you are only at the resort for a week or so.

However, if you do decide to use a children's program, remember to check it out thoroughly. Who are the counselors? Are the activities and equipment safe and appropriate for a toddler? What is the ratio of counselors to children? (One counselor to about every five toddlers would be good.) A mother recalls this extreme experience: "I was staying at a dude ranch with my three-year-old. In the morning when my husband and I went out riding I put him in a crowded children's program. We returned one day to hear that our son had strayed off quietly for a walk in the desert! It took the counselor half an hour to find him!"

It's a good idea for parents to stay with their toddler the first day. When you say good-bye, leave a phone number or at the least a location where the counselor can find you. I recommend that you ask the counselors to call you if your child is having any difficulty adjusting.

Sometimes parents or a baby-sitter decide to stay with a toddler who doesn't separate easily for the entire program. Both the child and the grown-up can find it more enjoyable to play with a group of children and adults than to dig sand castles alone at the beach all morning.

Staying with Relatives

Visiting relatives can be a wonderful way for family members to get close to one another. But the trip can be a disaster if parents and relatives aren't realistic. I recommend phoning Grandma or Uncle Sam before you arrive and being straightforward about your toddler's habits. If you explain that she wakes up at 5 A.M., often cries out in the middle of the night, and can't seem to sit still for more than five minutes at any meal, and your relatives insist they still want you, go for it!

While your relatives will probably volunteer to do some baby-sitting, be sure to reciprocate. Take your toddler out of the house alone for a few hours a day. This will not only give your relatives a break but it will let you and your toddler have some special time alone. Respect the rules of the house. For instance, if Grandma doesn't like people putting their feet on her coffee table, don't let your toddler do it. Many parents suggest having one meal alone daily with their toddler, whether at a restaurant or just at an earlier hour. Three meals a day with a two-year-old can be hard to digest even for the most loving relatives.

Traveling by Air

Before buying your tickets, call the airlines and ask how they accommodate children. Many have bins of toys and special children's snacks, but you usually have to request these things in advance. If possible, reserve the roomy bulkhead seats. Says one mother: "My daughter crawled into a cocoon in front of my feet and slept for almost the entire eight-hour flight."

You never know when your luggage could get sent on a slow voyage to China. Take a carry-on bag containing your toddler's necessities for three days or so. It also helps to bring some of your toddler's favorite snacks for the airplane ride. It may be that the only foods served are honeyed peanuts and brie, both of which your toddler passionately hates! One mother says she packs a special picnic with dozens of little wrapped foods—peanut butter sandwiches, animal crackers, dried apricots, string cheese. Her toddler spends almost the entire trip unwrapping and eating.

Your toddler might barely notice the air pressure as the plane takes off and lands if you are well stocked with lollipops and bottles. Fifteen minutes of sucking won't make your child a sugar addict for life but will help keep her ears from popping uncomfortably.

A toy and book bag is necessary for survival. Try surprising your child with new toys and books, as well as including some of his old favorites. Playing with puppets, putting stickers on airline cups, crayons and markers, and reading stories will help keep you from having to entertain your toddler by walking up and down the aisles.

If possible, schedule the flights to coincide with your child's bed- or nap times. If you have the choice of a flight with a layover or a nonstop flight, go for the nonstop alternative.

Traveling by Car

This is not the year to plan a drive cross-country. In fact, unless your child shuts his eyes the instant the car starts moving, I wouldn't drive much more than two hours per day. (If you have a long ride you might try driving at night while your toddler is sleeping.)

Toddlers usually love family sing-alongs. Take a stack of tapes of music that both you and your toddler like. Play simple games; for example, have your toddler point out all the red cars or all the trucks on the road. Snack stops are essential.

How to Plan Your Day

If you spent the morning at an antique fair, plan on spending the afternoon at the beach. Your toddler needs to have some fun too.

It is crucial to be realistic and flexible. If your child suddenly dissolves in a fit of crankiness when you are standing in line for a popular local restaurant have a fallback. What about buying sandwiches at a deli and having a picnic on a pier? Some parents tell me that if they do one small activity a day for themselves they are satisfied. Says one mother: "As long as I can do my forty-five-minute exercise video, I'm content to be there for my family the rest of the day."

Be sure to build in some rest and quiet playtime to your schedule every day. Sticking to your child's home schedule for nap time, bedtime, and mealtime will make life easier for her and for you. Your toddler is going to burn out if you rush her from one activity to another. Even two-year-olds get sick of zoos!

You know your child. He may love surprises or he may hate the slightest variation from his schedule. Says one mother: "The worst family trip we had was when Sara was three. We were just too loose about plans, sleeping in a different place almost every night. Sara needed more routine and seemed constantly irritable. Now when we go away, we stay put in one location and have very low-key days."

Baby-sitters

Even on family vacations parents need breaks. In fact, many parents say they've had their best vacations when they've brought along a friendly, energetic teenager or college student. A full-time caregiver will probably need your vacation time to get his or her own break.

Grandparents, aunts, and uncles can be welcome additions to a family's baby-sitting schedule. Vacationing together can also be a nice way for different generations of a family to spend some happy times together. Says one mother: "I wouldn't dream of taking a vacation without my parents. They love spending time with the kids and we get a break."

Depending on your relatives' tolerance and your family's need for privacy, they may decide to stay with you or find separate accommodations. A grandfather who rents his own room in a hotel near his daughter's summer house explains: "I wouldn't consider staying with my grandchildren in the house they rent for one week every summer. While I love spending time with them, I've had enough after a few hours. I like to read the paper in the sun and relax. It wouldn't be a vacation for me if I stayed in the house with them."

Many hotels and resorts offer baby-sitting services. You will want to spend some time with the baby-sitter and check references. If you are going to stay at one hotel, try to use the same baby-sitter every day.

Breaking Habits

Some parents use vacations to toilet train their toddler, wean him from the bottle, or work on getting him in tip-top shape. Says one mother: "When I took a vacation I suddenly saw my toddler in a new light. I never realized how difficult it was for him to be in a new situation. I spent so much of the trip trying to get him to be less cautious." Working parents, in particular, often see this concentrated time as a good opportunity to break habits.

Remember though, that this is a vacation. You want to enjoy your child. Don't view the vacation as a failure if your child doesn't return toilet trained or if she still jumps up and down at mealtimes. What's most important is to use the vacation as a time to get close to your toddler and possibly begin new ways of connecting. Don't expect miracles.

Summary

Some of the best memories you can give your family are those of your vacations together. However, don't let your expectations clash with the reality that you are vacationing with young children and will be on call at least as much as you are at home.

Better to plan a low-key one-stop trip rather than a whirlwind tour of the New England coastline. Better to have a cottage with a kitchen and outdoor activities at your beck and call than a luxury hotel suite in Paris.

Every family has its own priorities and needs. But you still have to find out if the trip is going to be appropriate for your toddler. For instance, one of my parent groups vetoed Disney World as too scary for a toddler. If there is a children's program attached to your vacation resort, check it out thoroughly. You need to decide if the separation will be too difficult for your toddler.

Remember, toddlers feel safe with routines. Don't neglect naps or regular mealtimes just because you are camping in the back woods of Michigan.

Many parents see their toddler in a new light on vacations and even use the time to break habits, such as bottle drinking, or to begin toilet training. But most important, a vacation is a great time to strengthen family ties.

▼ ▼ ▼ ▼ ▼ ▼ ▼ ▼ ▼ ▼ ▼ ▼ ▼ ▼ ▼ ▼ ▼ ▼

CHAPTER 15

Taking a Vacation Alone

S
O YOU WANT TO GO AWAY WITHOUT YOUR TODDLER! AS you may have already noticed, I believe that happy, contented parents make for happy, contented children. What could be wrong with a long weekend alone to remember why you married your partner? Renewing your life together as a couple can work wonders. Says one mother of a two-and-a-half-year-old: "With our long hours at work and the demands of being a parent, sometimes it feels as though we barely have a normal conversation in months, let alone physical contact! It is frightening to think how quickly my husband and I become distant. On our four days away we couldn't believe how much we enjoyed being with each other. The brief time alone gave our marriage a boost."

Of course, the one essential is to leave your child with a person whom you trust and whom he likes.

When to Tell Your Child

Since a toddler doesn't have much of a sense of time, why tell him about your vacation before you've even begun to pack? A few days before you leave, briefly present your trip as a fact of life. "Mommy and Daddy are going on vacation for three days. Grandma is going to stay with you. We will call you every day."

A vacation is not the time to break in a new baby-sitter or an unfamiliar grandparent. You want your child on her usual comfortable routine with people she sees regularly. If she's going to stay at Grandma's house, make sure she's had some trial runs to get used to her new environment. Also, don't forget to bring along her necessities of life, such as her favorite stuffed dog and precious blanket.

Preparations

While the recommendations here can be time-consuming (particularly as you try to pack and take care of a toddler simultaneously), they will help your toddler feel that his mother and father haven't forgotten him.

1. Put on your smock and get to work drawing pictures of your upcoming vacation—the airplane, the hotel, the beach.

2. Take a photo of your family together. Post the photo on the refrigerator or anywhere else where it will be easy for your toddler to spot.

3. If you are going away for more than a week, make a tape recording of you reading her favorite story or have someone videotape you. (Don't worry about rehearsing. Your toddler will think you are the best star in the world.)

4. Leave a calendar taped to the refrigerator and let your child cross off each day that you're away. (This activity will help your toddler understand that your vacation does have an end even though she doesn't yet get the concept of time.)

5. Make a daily chart of your child's schedule, what he eats, whom he plays with, and so on.

6. Alert your caregiver if your child has any recurrent illnesses, such as ear infections. She may not be missing you when she cries all the time. Her ears really may hurt!

7. Make sure that a neighbor has a set of your house keys.

8. In addition to leaving emergency phone numbers of the police, doctor, and relatives, leave the number where you can be reached. (You can rest assured that your two-year-old won't be phoning constantly at 6 A.M. After all, she doesn't know how to dial!)

9. Phone frequently.

The Real Thing

How do you really feel about going away alone? Parents who travel for work may feel terrible when they leave their child, but they usually have no choice in the matter. No one, however, is twisting your arm to take a vacation alone. Some parents feel so guilty about heading off for a much needed break that they tell their toddler they are going away for work! Says one father: "It was so difficult to tell my daughter that I was going on a vacation! My first instinct was to make up an excuse for being away. After all, I spend so much time away from her already. Shouldn't I be giving all my spare time to her?"

You have to give yourself permission to have a good time and get in touch with the adult part of yourself again. Remember, your toddler will be fine if he is left with someone who loves him and can care for him.

Plan on at least three days away. The first day you may still be on your child's time—looking at your watch and wondering what she is having for lunch or when she is taking a nap. You might not be able to believe that you don't have her breakfast dribbled on your shirt and that you are without your appendage when you stroll down the street. You'll need the two extra days to completely unwind and feel you are on vacation.

Routines and Special Treats

You want your child to know that life can go on as usual, even when his mother and father are off basking on some beautiful Caribbean beach. If Liz sees Sam on Tuesdays for a playdate, make sure that his caregiver keeps the date. If Freddy usually reads *Pat the Bunny* five times before dinner, ask his caregiver to let him read the book five times.

This can be a good opportunity for grandparents or close friends to take your child somewhere special, like the zoo. You want your toddler to have sweet memories of her vacation away from her mother and father!

How Long?

Toddlers may not be able to keep track of time hour by hour, day by day. But a long vacation may be painful for both your child and you. Five days away from your toddler will probably work out fine, but I wouldn't go around the world for three weeks.

If your toddler normally spends the entire day with a caregiver, a five-day vacation is probably not going to be as difficult for him as it would be for a child who is rarely separated from his parents.

▼ ▼ ▼ ▼ ▼ ▼ ▼ ▼ ▼ ▼ ▼ ▼ ▼ ▼ ▼ ▼ ▼ ▼ ▼ ▼
When Not to Go

1. After the birth of a sibling.

2. After any stressful event, such as moving or starting a new playgroup.

3. After a parent has been very busy at work.

4. The height of separation anxiety occurs at around eighteen months of age and then again at twenty-seven months. If possible, try to limit your time away during these periods.

▲ ▲ ▲ ▲ ▲ ▲ ▲ ▲ ▲ ▲ ▲ ▲ ▲ ▲ ▲ ▲ ▲ ▲ ▲

Remember, your child is a toddler only once. Her mother and father are the dearest things in her universe. It can be painful if you take too many vacations without her.

When You Return

When you run through the door with your arms wide open and a larger than life teddy bear that took up an entire seat on the plane, don't be surprised if you aren't given the royal welcome. Your toddler may very well run for cover behind his grandpa or the caregiver. Your toddler may shout, "Go away!" when you try to plant the tiniest kiss on his cheeks.

Try not to take such rejection personally. Some children need time to readjust to having their parents home. For example, one three-year-old boy wouldn't let his mother put him to sleep for the first two nights. He wanted his grandpa.

A ROMANTIC MOMENT

"I bet Shannon's taking her nap now."

Other toddlers store up their emotions of anger, sadness, and loneliness so successfully when their parents are away that they just can't hold their feelings in any longer. Now it is their turn to punish the deserters. A two-and-a-half-year-old who seemed perfectly happy with her caregiver when her parents were away barely spoke to her mother and father for three days except to say: "I'm going on a vacation. You stay home."

Parents need to be reassuring, to catch up on their child's routine, and to spend time with her. The very fact that you are now home and taking over her care should soon soothe your toddler.

Summary

A happy, relaxed parent will have a happy, relaxed child. Taking a vacation without your toddler may be one way to ensure his well-being in the long run.

Before heading off on your trip, you should make certain preparations. It's important to leave your toddler with someone she loves and trusts, who knows her regular routine. Try making a tape recording of you reading her favorite story or leaving written postcards to be given out as mail every day to your toddler.

Remember, after parents come home, their toddler may take some time to warm up and adjust. Don't take it personally.

▼ ▼ ▼ ▼ ▼ ▼ ▼ ▼ ▼ ▼ ▼ ▼ ▼ ▼ ▼ ▼ ▼ ▼ ▼

CHAPTER 16

Choosing Preschool and Daycare

THROUGHOUT THIS BOOK WE'VE TALKED ABOUT THE socialization of a child under the age of three. He screams, he grabs, he lives in the moment. The good news is that at around three years of age a child starts to settle down and becomes increasingly reasonable. He is finally more accepting of limits and easier to live with.

With toddlerhood behind him, a child is ready for more formal play experiences with children his own age on a daily basis. Whereas he might have been king of the mountain in his own backyard, he can now start working within a group. Sharing, negotiating, and empathizing become part of his social skills. He learns to trust adults outside his home.

When looking for a preschool or daycare center, it's crucial to find one your family feels comfortable with. You want a school or daycare center that's consistent with your home environment. For those parents who have already selected daycare for their child at an earlier age, this principle is always worth reviewing. For example, if

"Wait, Mr. Smith!"

you are low-key and don't place much emphasis on structured activities, you'll probably be happier with a liberal school where the child has more of a say in planning her day. If you are a very formal and highly organized person, you may prefer the more teacher-directed activities found in a traditional school.

An honest discussion of what you expect from the preschool or daycare center and your own introspection about your past experience as a student will help you clarify your feelings when you choose.

But whether parents choose traditional or liberal, full-time daycare or half-day preschool, the environment should be one that is warm and nurturing, where the child comes first and the parents are welcomed. When you make the rounds, be sure to visit the classrooms. It is most important to get a feel for the school or center and its atmosphere. You can only achieve this by observing a class in progress. It's also important to meet the director because she sets the overall tone and you should feel comfortable with her or him.

Word of mouth from friends or pediatricians is often the best referral. Does your town or city have a directory of preschools or daycare centers? Just as you would educate yourself about anything you buy as a consumer, you should educate yourself about pre-schools and daycare centers. See several schools or centers in your area. You want to have an overall knowledge that will enable you to make good general comparisons.

Many parents talk about how important it is to find the best preschool or daycare center near their home. Getting a three-year-old up, ready, and out in the morning is no easy matter. Says one mother: "I signed my son up for what was the most prestigious nursery school in the city. I didn't even think about the fact that it would take us forty minutes and two different buses to get there. After one year I couldn't stand the stress of getting to his school on time and enrolled in a school four blocks away."

This chapter offers certain guidelines to consider when deciding on a preschool or daycare center. Some apply more to preschool, others to daycare. Although no school or center will comply with all the suggestions, we felt it important for parents to have a frame of reference when asking questions and making a decision.

What to Look For When You Visit Preschools and Daycare Centers

Is the school or center licensed? Being licensed means that teachers' credentials, children's medical records, fire precautions, the building's condition, and the ratio of adults to children are double-checked. For example, in New York City there must be at least two teachers if there are more than ten three-year-olds in a group.

How large is the room? Do the room and toys look cared for, clean, and well organized?

Is there a safe outdoor environment? How often do the children go outdoors? They should have some large motor activity at least once a day.

Does the class have a refrigerator for snacks? Is water available to drink during the day along with juice at snack time?

Does the school or center have a dress code? Rough-and-tumble clothes allow a child to move freely and not worry about getting dirty.

Does the school or center require a complete change of clothes to make your child feel comfortable if she soils what she has on?

What is the policy on accidents? Are you called immediately, whether you are at home or work?

Does the school or center require you to phone if your child isn't coming to school?

Does the school or center require written permission from the parents if a child is being picked up by someone who doesn't usually come for him?

Are there enough developmentally appropriate activities for your child within the room? Is there a dress-up corner for fantasy, a play kitchen, blocks, a book corner, and toys that emphasize fine motor skills, such as puzzles? Does each class offer a variety of arts and crafts experiences, such as creating collages and finger painting?

Is the room a happy chaos? Do all children seem generally busy and relaxed? Is there a well-organized but natural rhythm to the day—a busy, somewhat noisy atmosphere during free play and then calm time for snack and stories?

Does the school or center have a policy on how to discipline a child? (I believe that discipline should be used as a teaching experience. A time-out accompanied by an explanation is reasonable, whereas humiliating a child by screaming at her is not.)

Is every child greeted by name and made to feel comfortable in the classroom?

Does the school or center have a special time for music and dance? Are there guinea pigs or snails to teach understanding of the mysteries of the animal world?

Is there a time when children sit together as a community to share news from home, making a child feel that home and school work well together? Circle time is democracy in its early stage.

How to Look at the Teachers

What are the teachers' credentials? Are the teachers trained in cardiopulmonary resuscitation and first aid?

How do the teachers resolve disputes between children? Do they interfere or do they let them resolve disagreements on their own as much as possible?

Do the teachers in the room complement each other in personality?

Do the teachers look each child attentively in the eye?

How enthusiastic are the teachers?

Do the teachers listen to each child?

Are each child's comments acknowledged?

Since every class has a variety of personalities, do the teachers pay appropriate attention to the shy, retiring child as well as to the aggressive, outgoing child?

Do the teachers pay more attention to one sex than the other?

Do the teachers seem to have a calm, easygoing way with the children?

How the Preschool or Daycare Center Involves Parents

How much does the school or center involve the parents? Are parents expected to participate in functions and meetings? Does the school or center offer workshops for parents and caregivers? Does the school or center accommodate working parents? Is this a community you feel comfortable with?

Are parents allowed to visit the classrooms often? Do you feel welcome?

Can you talk to the personnel, and are specialists available should you have a problem?

How many parent-teacher conferences are scheduled each year?

Is the policy to call parents immediately when there is a problem, and are you expected to inform the school or center about any difficulty that you may know of?

Will the school or center help you learn about future schools for your child?

What is the policy on birthday parties? At some schools, if you invite more than half the class you have to invite the whole class.

The Separation Process

Preschool or daycare will be one of the first of many separations from your beloved child. You may be surprised to find that you are flooded with your own memories of past school experiences and how you felt when your parents left you for the very first time.

Every preschool and daycare center should have specific procedures for helping a child separate and say good-bye to her parents. With a philosophy in place, it is much easier for families to decide where they feel comfortable.

For instance, at the Toddler Center we require that parents stay with their toddler for the first four weeks of school. Then we individualize according to each child's needs. If a child has difficulty separating, we may bring in both parent and child for a special play session.

Does the school or center have a general meeting to greet all parents and discuss how teachers handle separation?

Do the teachers make a home visit before the child starts at the school or center or during the separation period? A home visit helps your child connect his home with his school.

Does the school or center have a slow phasing-in process during which the children gradually increase their time at school?

What is the policy regarding parents' staying in the classrooms? It can take a long time for a child to feel comfortable.

Does the school or center understand and enable the parents to feel safe about leaving their child? This may mean that some parents stay longer than usual.

Do the teachers articulate the child's feelings when her parents leave and then help get the child busy in a new activity? For instance: "I see you're feeling sad because your mommy and daddy have left. They'll be back. Have you tried these new paints yet?"

Do the teachers phone your child when he has missed more than a few days of school?

If your child needs a little extra reassurance, is there a teacher available to comfort and help her through this tough time?

Summary

Preschool or daycare is probably the first experience your child will have of a life of his own without his mother, father, or caregiver. It pays for parents to do their homework and carefully investigate the atmosphere and safety of the preschool or daycare center they choose. I would recommend looking at several schools or centers and speaking to friends about why they chose one over another. Most preschools and daycare centers will schedule an informational visit to discuss general philosophy and curriculum.

It's helpful not only to tour the school but also to spend some time observing in the classrooms. Generally, you want to consider issues of safety, accreditation, and how the teachers see their role and respond to the children. The preschool's or daycare center's method of handling the separation process is important, and you should feel comfortable with it.

Made in the USA
Charleston, SC
22 March 2012